CHAPT

What is the meaning of life? Ah, the big question. Who are we? Why are we here? What is our purpose? The answers to these questions seem unattainable to most. When I was a young man I was so startled by the realization that nobody knew the answers to these questions that I became obsessed with pursuing the answers. I thought, "How could this be? How could people be running around clueless every day? How could you do something as important as, let us say, *life* and not know why you are doing it?" It shocked me into an otherworldly place of disbelief and single-mindedness. I simply could not wrap my head around the idea that we had to live life without direction, without purpose, without meaning.

Regardless of your opinion on whether this question can be answered or not, consider for the moment how strange it is that most of us go through life without a clue as to why we are even here. We are the most profound example of the blind leading the blind. Billions of people are wandering around on this rock in the middle of an expanse-which apparently extends in every direction into infinity-without the foggiest idea of how we got here or why. Yet, regardless of the fact that we don't have a clue as to why we are here and what it is we are meant to accomplish, we rise from bed every morning, go to school, work, fall in love, have children, and die. Yet, nobody knows why.

Although our world is unexplainable and actually inconceivable, we swagger through our day as if we were fully aware of our purpose. We are so accustomed to not knowing why we are here that most of us don't even ask the question. We live and die without ever expecting to know why we are all living and dying.

It is as if we have all agreed to some kind of genealogical silence. Many aren't even aware that they suffer from any ignorance at all. They go from childhood to adulthood in some Stepford-like trance without ever realizing they don't know the meaning of life.

Since we were children we have been reared to concern ourselves with other questions such as, "how to be successful" and "how to be happy." Nobody ever mentioned, "Oh, by the way nobody knows why we are here or what we're supposed to do with this life. But, in the absence of knowing why we are here we have manufactured a purpose called 'seeking success'." Yet, no one seems to notice that this is a substitute purpose. The facts regarding our existence are not only not known but also almost never even discussed. This type of conversation is reserved for teenage buddies to alternate between bong hits or for the small fraction of society who took a philosophy class in college.

We have become so comfortable with our ignorance regarding our existence that ignorance is the norm. Most people don't awake one day and tell their kids "you should be aware that nobody knows why were all alive, so in the absence of knowing what life is for, we have all decided to spend our lives pursuing the greatest amount of pleasure we can find." Instead of having this conversation we just teach our kids as much as we can about how to find pleasure. Our entire school system is directed to give our kids the basic tools so they can get a job so they can make a living so they can buy stuff and have a family. Why do they do this? Because we think that by having these things it will make them happy. Life has become an imaginary race for the trophies of physical comfort and objects of pleasure.

Life is a long day at the racetrack. The education system is the kennel where the greyhounds are trained for the big race. For thirteen years we teach our children the tools they will need in order to pursue and catch the rabbit of "success." And upon graduation they are let out of the chute and off they go. Some dogs catch the rabbit and get the big doghouse by the sea while others who came from the less funded public schools get a modest doghouse in the valley.

You may disagree that we are all ignorant about the reason for our existence. You may be saying to yourself that the religions tell us why we are here and therefore we are not as ignorant as I suggest. But if you look a little closer you will see that the religious institutions don't really tell us *why* we are here but rather they tell us *what* we should do now that we are here. Christianity tells us that some "guy" named God put us here and now that you are here you should be good to others, keep the commandments, and believe in the God that put you here. But if you look closely it never explains *why* this God put us here. The

4

other religions tell a similar story about what to do now that we are here but have the same omission regarding the purpose of our creation.

Let me ask you this: how do we know if someone is "successful" in life if we don't know what she was meant to accomplish? We admittedly don't know why we are here but claim to know when someone was successful at life. In reality, what we are saying is that in the absence of knowing why we are here we have constructed arbitrary "goals," and if you accomplish them, we will deem you successful. And, oddly enough, if you ask someone if they believe the meaning of life is to accumulate wealth and personal pleasure, they will typically say "Oh, no!" as if that was obviously an immature and vain way to spend life. But, immediately following their dismissal of that proposition they will turn away from you and resume their life of accumulating wealth and personal pleasure.

The fact of the matter is that we pursue wealth because we believe it will give us the experiences that bring us pleasure and we do it because we have never been shown any other path or worthy endeavor to use our life for. Therefore, why would we do anything else with our life? No secular or religious institutions have ever given us anything else to sink our teeth into.

I believe that there comes a time in the life of a soul when it "wakes up," looks around and says, "Hey, wait a minute, there is something wrong with this picture. Why am I doing this? There has to be more to life than to enter the stressful race of trying to fight for my piece of the pie only to have it all taken away at death anyway."

About thirty-five years ago, when I was a young man, I began to wonder about the meaning of life. I thought that there had to be more to life than what the world was offering. I wanted to know why I was alive. So, I set out in pursuit of the meaning of life and it has been quite an adventure.

I told myself I would try anything and listen to anybody who had something to offer on the subject of life and its purpose. I tried drugs, studied philosophy, lived like a monk on a commune, went to college and got a degree in theology. I traveled around the world, went to graduate school and got a law degree, escaped to the mountains for several years and meditated, moved to the city to see what was going on, had several "real" jobs, many "wacky" jobs: I worked 2000' underground as a zinc miner in New Jersey, I was a carpenter in Montana, a waiter, bartender, bicycle messenger, and civil rights investigator in Chicago, an attorney in Denver, a cab driver in Los Angeles. I started twelve different companies, employed hundreds of people. I moved around the country, I backpacked around the world, I rode a bicycle across the United States, I prayed, meditated, drank a lot of beer. I read many books, practiced different religions, fell in love, got married, had children, questioned everything, made many mistakes and had many incredible spiritual experiences.

At times I have felt disillusioned, confused, and lost. I've often wondered, "Why couldn't I just go with the flow and go get a job, manufacture, sell or service something, purchase my stock options, pack away my 401(k), and look forward to tomorrow?" But, the drive to find out life's purpose was too strong. "I'm on a mission from God," I would tell myself with a hint of laughter.

I decided that it was to be my life's purpose to find these answers. Not a day passed without me acknowledging that promise. I realize how bold this must sound but after a thirty-five-year search I found the meaning of life. Believe it or not I could sum it up in a couple of sentences. Explaining it is not difficult. Embodying it might be the hardest challenge ever presented to human beings. Although it takes no great intelligence to grasp nor any great strength to accomplish, it will amaze you how your whole being will scream out in objection and resistance. And that is why I cannot simply blurt it out. I promise I will reveal it in its entirety, but without the proper preparation your mind, if it is anything like mine, will fight it.

If you have the courage to question the way you currently look at the world, I can show you the way. If you can summon the strength to resist some mental and emotional habits that have dragged you through life, I can help you break free from fear, anxiety, and depression and show you a world of unending happiness and peace.

The strangest thing about my pursuit of the meaning of life was the unintended and amazing side effects. Even if my conclusion regarding what the meaning of life is does not answer every esoteric question you have, I guarantee that it will improve almost every aspect of your life by simply practicing a couple of my suggestions.

As I stated previously, my goal in life was to find life's deepest meaning. I was "hell bent" on finding the true purpose of our existence. Living life was always a secondary endeavor. Not only did I find the meaning of life, but I also found a tremendously rewarding life free of stress, fear, and anxiety. I figured out how to enjoy being a loving spouse, a fearless entrepreneur, an attentive father, a caring friend, and the happiest person I know.

My goal in life was not to find the most enjoyable life I could ever imagine, but that is what happened along the way. That is simply the natural side effect of pursuing the meaning of life. If you want to rid yourself of financial stress, marital problems, professional issues, the fear of anything, etc. and exchange them for joy, bliss, and fearlessness, then please let me show you what I have found. It will not take me long to explain how to get there. How far you want to go and fast you want to get there will be completely up to you.

You may think that finding enlightenment is some huge undertaking that takes decades of dedication, meditation, and sacrifice. This could not be further from the truth. If you are willing to apply even a moderate amount of effort, you can become enlightened by the end of this book. I know that sounds impossible, but I swear to you it is true. I can easily explain enlightenment to you. All you need is an open mind.

Once you grasp enlightenment all of the positive side effects are at your disposal. I mean it. You can have all of it and you can do it all within this lifetime. I started this life as a poor Irish-Catholic raised on welfare in a "broken" home in the Bronx, NY with moderate intelligence. I was/am average in every way describable.

I am currently a very happy person, married to an amazing woman. I have two wonderful children, and I have learned to experience fearlessness and timelessness on demand. I was not trying to carve out the perfect life; it was an innocent, unintended, natural side effect of my pursuit of enlightenment.

It is important to note that in order to become enlightened you don't have to go anywhere. You don't have to give up anything. You don't have to change your name. You don't have to join some radical movement. All you need to do is understand a few simple concepts and then apply them to your life. And I promise you your life will become an amazingly peaceful, enjoyable, beautiful, fearless experience. Even if you do not care what the meaning of life is, then read on and let me show you how to enjoy life on a level not even contemplated in your average "get rich," "live great" book.

Let me take you on my personal journey in search of enlightenment in order to walk your psychology through the progression it takes to grasp enlightenment. I will explain this in great detail later but your mind, ego, does not want you to understand enlightenment. Enlightenment leads to its death. If I blurt out these liberating concepts too soon, your ego will freak out. We need to trick it. Your ego does not want to die. It will resist this attempted assassination. You have to help me take down its defenses. Although it hears us talking about it right now it has no idea that we are plotting its takeover...its demise.

Let me entertain your ego with my story. I want to share how I was able to trick my ego and distract it just long enough for the truth to slip by this formidable gatekeeper. Let me explain how I discovered my ego, fought it, lived with it, made deals with it, laughed at it, and eventually realized it is my worst enemy and my greatest teacher. My hope is that through the story of my life that is woven into this book you will see how my ego's control over my life gradually lessened, how we must dance our way out of this destructive relationship, and how each step of liberation brings such great rewards...brings enlightenment.

Throughout my journey I've been misled, and I have misled. I have seen great compassion and the worse of human judgment. At times I have been very lazy while other times I have amazed myself at my determination and resolve to sit still and meditate even deeper. I have had longs periods where I was unable to enjoy even the slightest spiritual experience and others where I thought I would never come back. I have experienced complete bliss and timelessness. I have had spiritual experiences you would find hard to believe. I have met extremely enlightened people who helped me find my way. And over time I began to hear a voice and feel a presence all around me. And I began to realize what I have always suspected: that there is much more to life than I was told. This is my story.

The Path

My friend, there is no solitude so drear as he hath who is in the world, but not of it. Wilt thou venture onwards, braving this peril? At this point there is yet a chance of return without incurring the danger which follows when further advanced. Set not thy hand to the plow if thou canst not go to the end of the furrow; it is long and difficult to follow. The world hath not so hard a task as this to impose in all its power. I offer thee option.

A Dweller on Two Planets, pg. 147

CHAPTER TWO

My search began with the questions that enter a kid's mind as they are growing out of adolescence. I was living in northern New Jersey with my six brothers and sisters, my mom, and stepfather. We were your average lower middle-class, East Coast, second-generation Irish immigrant, Catholic church-attending, well meaning, loving, dysfunctional family. My search towards finding the meaning of life started early due to the fact that I was blessed with a very inquisitive mother who had returned to college to get a degree in philosophy just as I was becoming a teenager.

I cannot tell you how many days I spent sitting around the kitchen table eating my cheerios while my mother would be spouting off some philosophical concept. She would be saying things like, "I think; therefore I am," and stuff about how "morality is not a universal truth but rather a human creation". Yada yada yada. I was always thinking this stuff is all interesting

14

and cool and everything but why doesn't she just tell me what the meaning of life is? When is she going to let me in on the big secret? I'm not a kid anymore. I'm ready for the big answer.

At that point in my life, I assumed that the only reason I didn't know the meaning of life was because I was a kid, and when I was old enough, my mom would explain it to me. I figured it was on the parental list of things to tell the kids when they got old enough and she had been too busy to get around to it. You know the list: 1) where babies come from; 2) how to change a flat tire; 3) how to tie a necktie; 4) how to find the right spouse; 5) what the meaning of life is, etc.

Well, one day, while sitting patiently through another interesting philosophical conversation, an incredibly frightening thought crept into my head. "Maybe my mom hasn't told me the meaning of life yet because she doesn't know what the meaning of life is." Then I thought, "That's ridiculous. Of course she knows the meaning of life." As I have said earlier, how could anyone do anything, especially something relatively important like, let's say, LIFE, for forty years without knowing why she is doing it? It didn't make sense. So I simply came out and asked her. "So mom, all

THE MEANING OF LIFE: ONE MAN'S JOURNEY AND DISCOVERY OF LIFE'S MOST IMPORTANT QUESTION

this philosophical mumbo jumbo about the origin of morals and different perspectives on how to treat each other are real interesting and everything but "WHY ARE WE HERE? I'm old enough now. What's the scoop?"

I shoveled another spoonful of Cheerios to my mouth and waited for her answer. I was expecting her to begin with "Well, a very long time ago God decided it would be good for the universe if we all came here and worked together to (blah blah blah), so that's why we are here. But, to my great horror, that did not happen. She looked at me with a puzzled expression, as if I was asking some off the wall question or something. Then she began to speak and out of her mouth came the most bizarre thing I have ever heard to this day. She said, "Uh, humm...Well, nobody knows why we are here."

All of a sudden I was thrown into the middle of a Twilight Zone episode. I was like "WHAT! What! Are you crazy, that's impossible!!! That can't be true. There are billions of people living here and billions upon billions that have come before us. Someone must have figured out why we are here by now. She has to be joking." Then I looked at her and realized that she wasn't joking. Then I thought, "Oh my God, my poor mother must have had a nervous breakdown some time ago, and I've been trapped in this house with a madwoman. How could she say such a thing? It's crazy talk. Of course people know why they are alive. I mean, we sent people to the moon and stuff. She has to be confused. She's forty years old; she must know why she is here by now. I mean, what the heck has she been doing all this time? How do you do anything for forty years and not know why you are doing it? This is crazy."

I felt like I just came upon someone building a huge pile of rocks and I said to them, "Hey buddy, what are you doing?"

And they responded, "Building a big pile of rocks."

"I see that wise guy, how long have you been at it?"

"Oh, about forty years."

"Wow," I would respond. "Let me ask you a crazy question...*WHY IN GOD'S NAME ARE YOU BUILDING A BIG PILE OF ROCKS?*"

And they would respond, "Oh, I don't know."

Then, still in this horrible dream, I look around and like a bizarre Steven King novel the horizon is filled with people building piles of rocks. Each person trying to "out do" the other, stealing rocks from each other, warring over rocks, making alliances for rocks, etc. Yet, nobody knew why they were killing each other for the rocks. Why were they building their rock piles??? This is the problem with Steven King novels. They make you think of things like this.

So, back at the kitchen table, I began to realize that the woman who raised me, fed and protected me, and the one who was responsible for preparing me for life hadn't a clue as to what the heck we were all doing here. And, even worse, nobody knew. Apparently, they (meaning the adults) were still debating it.

I couldn't believe it. I mean, I just learned in school the other day that we haven't been monkeys for thousands of years. Now you mean to tell me that we still haven't figured out why the heck we are all here? What the hell has everybody been doing? Shouldn't we have answered this question first? I mean, we have teams of our smartest people spending billions of dollars trying to figure out how to genetically reproduce cats and dogs, which we already have an excess of, and nobody working on figuring out why we are all here. Am I the only one who thinks this is nuts???

So, there I sat at the kitchen table on 80 Summit Drive in lovely, Sussex, New Jersey, and I was in utter shock. I thought to myself, "You mean to tell me that I'm trapped on this planet with billions of people basically wandering around, bumping into each other without any idea what we are all doing here. No wonder we're so screwed up." (On a personal note, my mom didn't know how to change a tire, how to tie a necktie, and she definitely didn't know how to find a good spouse either. Apparently, she figured out the childbearing issue, but I'd rather not think about that.)

So I asked her, "What about that Jesus Christ guy I've heard so much about? Didn't he tell us why we are here?"

She said, "Not really. He focused more on what we should do now that we are here and what horrible things will happen to us if we don't take his advice."

"So," I asked, "what about the Buddha guy, you know that fat guy who invented incense, what did he have to say?"

She replied, "He pretty much did the same thing Christ did. He focused more on what we should do now that we are here. He really didn't talk about how or why we are here."

Then I asked, "What is everybody doing running around getting married, having kids, and going to work all day? What are they trying to accomplish?"

She said, "They're simply doing what they were taught to do. What else are they going to do? They don't know why we are here. Some of them may think they know. They will say things like, 'I'm here to be a good Christian,' or 'to treat people like I would like to be treated,' or 'to teach people about Jesus Christ.' But none of these statements explain *why* life was created but rather what to do with life now that you are here."

Let's forget about my mom trying to scare the shit out of little Jimmy for a moment. Can you recall as a teenager or any other time in your life when you realized that nobody knew why they were alive? that all of society suffered from a shared ignorance? Does this time stand out in your mind as a very momentous event, or am I the only wacky one this happened to?

Let me ask you another question. Do you really think that some "God" created us simply on the chance that we would be one of the lucky few who had their dinner interrupted one night by some group of overly zealous (and usually a bit wacky) people who informed us of the "good news" that God had a son? Wouldn't it have been easier if God simply created us with that information? We could have side-stepped this whole crazy mess. Who knows, maybe he forgot?

Anyway, back to the kitchen table where my mom was attempting to reduce her maternal responsibilities by one child by scaring little Jimmy right into the neighborhood insane asylum. "Wow," I thought. I mean...I couldn't believe it. You mean nobody knows why we're alive? "Well, do we have large groups of very smart people working on the issue who are very close to coming up with the answer?"

She replied, "Not that I know of."

Man, talk about the blind leading the blind. It seemed so strange. Every day we all walk by each other in the grocery store, marching along as if we are on some mission. Yet, we are all oblivious. Nobody has a clue as to what we are doing here or what we are really supposed to accomplish.

As I walked around my little town of Sussex, affectionately called "Sausage" by my friends, everyone looked relatively fine with the fact that no one knew why they were alive. So I began to wonder, should I join them? Should I dive into the fray? Thrust my head into the proverbial sand of our joint ignorance and go about "life?" Go get "that education" so I can be more qualified than my peers so I can get "that job" which will pay me more than others so I can get "those things" before everyone else gets them, so me and "my loved ones" can do "those things" which everyone wants to do in order to have a "successful and happy life"?

"But why?" I thought. It sure seems easier than the alternative, which would be to spend my life trying to answer a question that, apparently, no one else has been able to answer. But going about life without knowing why we are even here simply did not make sense. Did some omnipresent being really create us simply to see who would end up with the house by the sea? Is this some type of amazingly elaborate maze filled with white, black, Asian, and Latino mice all running around trying to hoard the cheese and procreate?

Trust me, I tried numerous times to get my head safely secured in the sand so I could begin spending my days competing against those around me for the stuff we were told we were supposed to be trying to get, but I just couldn't. I couldn't get the questions out of my head. I had no choice but to go a different route. So I eventually left lovely Sausage, New Jersey thirty-one years ago in search of the truth.

Analyze

Do not believe in anything simply because you have heard it. Do not believe in anything simply because it is spoken and rumored by many. Do not believe in anything simply because it is found written in your religious books. Do not believe in anything merely on the authority of your teachers and elders. Do not believe in traditions because they have been handed down for many generations. But after observation and analysis, when you find that anything agrees with reason and is conducive to the good and benefit of one and all, then accept it and live up to it.

— *Gautama Buddha*

CHAPTER THREE

I decided it would be best to start my quest for the ultimate answer with sex, drugs, and alcohol. How original! I tried drugs for the same reasons most other kids do, 1) because they were there, 2) I was bored, 3) it was fun, 4) I could have cool experiences without any real effort, and 5) it helped me deal with the stress of deciding what to do with my life. Remember, I was plagued with the crazy notion that I was to devote my life to discovering the meaning of life. That was hard to do when all the adults around me were asking, "Well, young man, what are you going to do with your life?"

And I would respond cautiously, "I really want to find out the meaning of life."

They would look at me wide-eyed with a look like I must be on drugs and say something like, "You know you can't make a living running around chasing fantasies young man." They would actually get irritated with me like I was messing with them. They seriously thought I was either an idiot or a wiseass.

Nobody seemed to know where someone would go if they wanted to find the meaning of life. That really wasn't one of the "career options" advertised at "Career Day" in my school's gymnasium. But I soon realized that I would need to pick the road I would travel in this life. The road straight ahead of me with all the flashing lights and fanfare read, "College: enter here and gain society's highest respect." On both sides of this road were Father-Knows-Best-type moms and dads, standing there, smiling gleefully, and cheering as a row of young men and women marched in a single file. All the young men wore their neatly pressed shirts with bow ties and the girls had on their skirts and saddle shoes. As they marched by, a distinguished looking older gentleman pounded a stamp on their foreheads that read "College bound."

That road was very tempting because it is what everyone wanted me to do. If I decided to go down that road, I would stop getting the looks of "you poor lost soul." I would often think to myself, "Come on, just hop in line and go to college and go along with the flow until you find something else to do." But then I would think, "Don't do it simply because it will be easier than dealing with all the judgment from people. I have to do what will help me understand why I am here. I have to stick to my guns and pursue my plan of finding out the meaning of life." I was so afraid I was going to wake up the next September and all my friends would have moved off to college and I would be in my mom's basement, staring at the wall and waiting for the meaning of life to come to me.

I knew I could not let that happen. There had to be other roads to choose from, and one of them was bound to lead me to the meaning of life. For a high school graduate there are several options. The college road is the most respected by society, and then there are the other alternatives. One road had a sign that read, "Enter here for union cards and blue-collar training." I tried this for a while, and when I wasn't either freezing my ass off or melting in the heat, I was too drunk to think about anything. Another read, "Housewives and Homemakers." I was disqualified for some obvious reasons. One read, "Artist." I have no artistic talents. Another, "Priest, Ministers, Rabbis Etc." Close, but not the lifestyle I could tolerate. Another, "Criminals, Druggies and Troublemakers." Close, but another lifestyle I could not tolerate.

Another, "Military Personnel Only." Definitely not the lifestyle I could tolerate. None of them seemed right for me. I thought that there must be another road. I had to keep looking. Where is the road for people who want to figure out the meaning of life? Which way do I go?

The pull towards the road to College was enormous. There was so much movement in that direction and such expectation surrounding it that for me to stop and even consider any other road was like resisting the pull of a black hole. I could hear people saying, "Come on, what are you stopping for? You're smart enough to do whatever you want. What are you thinking? Go for it. Get the degree, the great job, the beautiful wife, and take your piece of the pie."

If you tell people you are not going to college because you think it is more important to go find the meaning of life, they look at you as if you've been eating paint chips like Wheaties. Our society does not recognize that as a respectable endeavor. You are immediately considered flaky or psychologically unstable. You hear things like, "He must have had it rough growing up," or "I knew that kid was on drugs." The fact of the matter was that I did do drugs, but that was not why I wanted to spend my life looking for the meaning of life. It actually happened the other way around. One of the reasons I was doing drugs was because I wanted to look for the meaning of life but didn't know how, so, in the interim, I tried to amuse myself.

I was pulled between "being responsible" in the world's eyes which meant keeping in stride with the "path of success" i.e., go to college and the other road of holding on to that inner calling to go in search for more meaning regardless of what the world thought of me. I was so conflicted I just stopped. I could not enter any of the roads. I just froze in disbelief that there weren't any other choices in life. None of the choices before me seemed to fit. I just stopped and stood there in limbo and watched all my friends "starting their lives." I felt the pressure of "getting left behind." I heard the whispers of my elders, as they would say, "Isn't it a shame that that Tarpey kid isn't doing anything with his life. He *had* such potential." They made it sound like I was dead.

At one point, my plan was to work for a few months, scrape together some money, fly to India, wander off into the mountains, and look for a guru. Then I though a tiger probably would eat me within a few hours. There had to be a better way.

For two years I did odd jobs and basically loafed. I was a carpenter for a little less than a year. I liked being outside and the work was fun, but I was extremely bored. I smoked a lot of pot and was drunk on a regular basis. Then I worked in a zinc mine 2500 feet underground and I liked blowing up dynamite and driving the little train around, but I got fired for skipping work to go to the "Live Aid" concert in Philadelphia. After getting fired I took the money I made and backpacked around Europe for a couple of weeks with my brother and a close friend.

When I returned from Europe I began tending bar, which was the best job I had to that point. I couldn't believe someone would pay me to drink, socialize, and pick up women. But within a year I was once again bored, and my anxiety to do something with my life was growing too strong for even the drugs to dilute.

Around this time my stepfather (who, by the way, was an incredibly sweet man) was tragically electrocuted one day while at work. He was finishing up his last year of a thirty-year career as a "motorman"/train operator for the New York transit authority.

This only motivated me further to figure out how something so tragic could happen to such a nice guy only months before he was about to retire and enjoy his life. He worked so hard for all those years and looked so forward to retirement. I couldn't believe life could take him away so close to his goal of finally relaxing and enjoying himself.

After his death my mother decided to travel for a while. She went gallivanting around the country looking for a better life. She, too, was looking for the meaning of life and was eager to listen to anyone who had an opinion on the matter. After about six months she settled down in Boulder, Colorado because, as she put it, "There were a lot of spiritually minded people there." I went to visit her for Christmas 1987 and I was instantly enamored with Colorado's beauty, intrigued with Boulder's pompous intellectualism, and relieved to have any change to the life I had been living.

I immediately went back to New Jersey, said goodbye to all the regulars at the bar where I had been working, grabbed my stuff, and headed for the mountains. Boulder was full of shops with books and trinkets from all over the world. By the time I had

THE MEANING OF LIFE: ONE MAN'S JOURNEY AND DISCOVERY OF LIFE'S MOST IMPORTANT QUESTION

arrived my mom was already knee deep in tons of new philosophical and spiritual teachings.

At this point I decided that although college may not help me understand the meaning of life it probably wouldn't get in the way. So, I enrolled in classes at the University of Colorado. I figured the closest degree they offered towards finding the meaning of life was philosophy, so I that is what I signed up for. I was going to become a philosopher.

The Advice of Scholars

A group was enjoying the music at a Chinese restaurant. Suddenly a soloist struck up a vaguely familiar tune. Everyone recognized the melody but no one could remember its name. So they beckoned to the splendidly clad waiter and asked him to find out what the musician was playing. The waiter waddled across the floor, then returned with a look of triumph on his face and declared in a loud whisper, "Violin!"

The scholar's contribution to spirituality!

Teachings of Father Anthony DeMello

CHAPTER FOUR

So, I started studying philosophy. I didn't realize it at the time, but it became an extremely important part of my path toward discovering the meaning of life. Philosophy, according to Webster's Dictionary, "is the rational investigation of the truths and principles of being, knowledge, or conduct." It's the art of questioning everything. This, as you will see, is an essential tool if you are to discover the meaning of life.

Philosophical theories don't typically make conclusions regarding the meaning of life but rather they discuss the basis of the conclusion. One particular field many philosophers enjoyed analyzing was Religion. Religion, and all of its dogma, which is a principle or set of principles laid down by an authority as incontrovertibly true, is the perfect target for the philosopher. Whenever you claim that you have an "incontrovertible truth" you are begging for a philosophical fight. What inspired the philosophers even more was that the religious are particularly bad at being open to questioning their theology or other people questioning it. The philosopher may not tell you what the meaning of life is, but they are pretty good at pointing out some inconsistencies in your conclusions regarding what it is.

I was not offended by the attack on Religion. At this time in my life I somehow was convinced that religions were nothing more than a bunch of human-made concepts created to pacify people's fear of dying, or, even worse, it was a lucrative business selling the product of immortality to a bunch of frightened people. I grew up in a time when Jimmy and Tammy Baker were still on TV, and I could not believe people would give these idiots money. My favorite bumper sticker at the time read, "God: Save Me From Your Followers."

All the people I knew who claimed to be religious were annoyingly judgmental, pompous in their belief, elitist towards other faiths or those of no faith, and hypocritical to the very faith they claimed to hold so dear. I thought that if that was being religious, I didn't want any part of it. It had been my experience that these religious people would be just as likely to lie, cheat, steal, be mean to their neighbor, be unfaithful to their spouse, hate, seek revenge, and a myriad of other activities which they claimed their religions preached against.

This is the scary part for an intellectual. Many people believe that in order to step over into the "religious" or "spiritual" you must depart from reason and adopt faith as your guide. Well, this is not true. The day you discard your reason you will be hopelessly adrift. The step over into the spiritual is not a departure from reason but simply a different mindset regarding where to apply it.

There are millions of people in the world who want to live with their myths. It pacifies their fears. They want to believe in a God that will take care of them when they die. They can't prove this God exists, but they choose to believe in that God because the fear of the unknown is too strong to live with without some source of relief, even if that relief is mythical. I call it mythical because they cannot prove through reason that this God exists.

I had a psychology teacher in High School who once said to my class that the belief in God is nonsense. I am sure the administrators would not have appreciated this type of religion talk in a public high school, but it was a turning point in my understanding of human nature. He wasn't simply bashing religion, but, rather, his point was that all though the existence of a God cannot be detected by any of our senses, people choose to believe in a God anyway. He was defining nonsense as beliefs we have although we cannot confirm the rationale of those beliefs or the existence of the object of our beliefs by the use of our senses. Non-sense beliefs are nonsense. That was the day I began to consider the fact that maybe people simply choose to believe in a God because they like to believe in God and that maybe "he" doesn't exist. This was a profound and frightening moment for me.

Think of all the things that you must confront if you are going to entertain the idea that God doesn't exist. If there isn't some omnipresent being running the show, then who's driving this thing, this existence? Where are we going? What will happen to me when I die? You must ask, what would possess a majority of our society to want to believe in a myth? You start asking yourself are we as a people that frightened about our existence? If we are capable of believing in this manufactured reality, how many other aspects of our social beliefs, and therefore my life, are equally manufactured myths? I'm not now nor was I then advocating atheism but rather agnosticism, the courage to admit that we don't know. From that day on I couldn't allow myself to believe in things that I could not understand through reason.

My dislike for religion was not borne out of complete ignorance. I was raised Catholic and my family actually attended Church on a semi-weekly basis. I even attended catechism. For those of you who don't know what catechism is, it is a series of classes Catholics attend to learn about the Catholic faith. Therefore, religion wasn't a completely foreign creature to me, but what I did know seemed dogmatic and pedantic.

This dislike for religion was only intensified by my study of philosophy. Many philosophers argue that religions have been concocted by people in order to pacify their fear of the unknown or to gain social and political advantage over people by claiming to be the gatekeepers to an afterlife and the moral high ground. I had to admit that when you read about the evil deeds done in the name of religion and by those claiming to be religious you have to wonder if they actually believed in what they preach. The blatant hypocrisy of those who would preach "as you do unto the least of these my brethren you do unto me" and "love thy neighbor" and then go off and massacre 1,000s during the Crusades in a name of Jesus seems more a belief of convenience than genuine theology.

Although I was really enjoying exploring the mind's ability to question and deconstruct every aspect of social, political, moral, and theological disposition, I wasn't getting much closer to understanding the meaning of life. Rather, I was becoming more convinced that if anyone claimed to have discovered the meaning of life what probably happened was that their fear of not knowing why they were alive simply won over their rationality. In other words, they simply made up their belief or adopted someone else's belief in order to pacify their fear of not knowing why they are alive or their fear of death. Although my knowledge regarding various theological and philosophical concepts was increasing, so too was my belief that it was impossible to truly discover "a" meaning of life. So it was like one step forward and two steps back.

For me this was an important period in my spiritual journey. Philosophy is an incredibly important intellectual vehicle which can foster a tremendous amount of wisdom, but it is important to realize the limitations if applied only externally. Philosophy, you may recall, "is the rational investigation of the truths and principles of being, knowledge, or conduct." The key word in that definition is "rational." Rational is defined as "agreeable to or in accord with reason." Reason, as we know, is an act performed by the mind.

So, philosophy can be described as the practice of using our mind in order to find the "truth" about our being, our knowledge, and our conduct. The problem arises when this powerful tool is wholly directed and controlled by the problem itself: the ego. Image you are sailing off to fight your worst enemy, but, unbeknownst to you, the captain of your ship is one of your opponent's top generals. Regardless of how skilled a soldier you are, you will most likely fail because ultimate control of your journey rests in the hands of someone who doesn't want the outcome you are seeking. This enemy that lies within, the ego, will be discussed at great lengths in later chapters.

A great example of how the mind can assist us in understanding human conduct can be found in a book by Friedrich Nietzsche called, "The Genealogy of Morals." The book changed my life. Its basic premise is that morals have an origin and the origin is human-made. Morality is more of a social construction than a divine edict. Humans created the morals we live by because they wanted to create boundaries for acceptable behavior. This made life more predictable while also preserving a way of life by which the majority wanted to live. They simply labeled their way of looking at life the "moral way" so everyone else would feel obligated to live that way as well.

By forcing their view of life on society, it was easier for them to obtain the life they wanted because there was no opposing "force" or avenue of acceptable expression. It also made the moral majority feel more "righteous" about their desired way of approaching life. This is a great example how reason can assist us in understanding human conduct.

Many religious devotees argue that deconstructing our social assumptions through this form of reason is one thing, but can it help us understand how or why we exist? Can it help you explain how the universe expands in every direction into eternity? It can't. The brightest minds this world has ever known have tried to fully understand our existence, and they have failed. It is simply impossible to wrap the mind around the concept of eternity. The most basic question regarding our physical existence, or our "being," cannot be grasped via the philosophical process. Our very existence is too profound or too elaborate for the mind and our senses to grasp. Our mind cannot conceive of the universe never ending or, the converse, it ending. If it ended, then what is on the other side? Nothingness? We cannot conceive of eternity. Nor can we conceive of nothingness.

For this topic the religious are correct. The mind and, therefore, reason has its limitations. It may not be able to guide us to the full understanding of our physical existence, but can it root out fear, anxiety, depression, superstition, and reveal bliss? Let me ask you this, would you rather understand how a black hole works or be blissfully happy all of the time? Which outcome would be more beneficial to your day-to-day experience?

You may be asking, "If the philosophical science is so powerful at finding bliss why are almost all philosophers pompous, depressed, angry jackasses?" This is a very good question. As an example let's explore the work of the Russian philosopher, Feodor Dostoevsky. His ability to tear apart even the subtlest human assumption was astounding. It was as if his mind moved so much faster than the average person that he was able to make many more observations regarding life than a normal person. This enabled him to catch an aspect of a social or psychological nuance that the average person would miss. When you read his writings you see a genius who has so aptly dissected life that he has uncovered the truth regarding our existence and that truth is that our existence is not rational. Or, in other words, our existence cannot be understood by the mind via this process of analyzing it. How did we all end up on this rock in the middle of an existence we are not able to comprehend? And how is it that we can go about life without understanding how or why we are here? The guy was a genius. His only flaw was that he failed to properly use his great powers of rationale upon himself.

Imagine if you needed water and you began to dig in a location where there simply was no water. Regardless of how intelligent you are or how hard you dig, your efforts will be fruitless. Dostoevsky didn't lack the tools. Like I said, he was a genius. But if you apply your power of rationale upon the wrong subject, you will not get the answers you seek. The answer to happiness is not in the world around us but rather in the world within us.

Religious prophets are typically philosophers that directed their power of reasoning inward. Most philosophers either don't have the courage to direct their steely criticism upon themselves, or they don't have the will to undergo that type of scrutiny. It is much easier to gaze upon the world with dissecting judgment, but to turn that attention inward and begin your own personal autopsy requires a resolve that most never command.

Like many philosophers there became a time when I felt like I hit a glass ceiling. It seemed that simply judging the way the world functioned was taking me down endless roads of critique but not to any concrete direction or purpose. My reasoning was breaking down my beliefs and socially learned ideas but it wasn't replacing them with better ones. I felt like I was becoming a wiped chalkboard. What I craved was meaning and "correct" information and not just liberation from dogma.

This is where the philosopher and the religious seemed to conflict. The religious have a myriad of beliefs that require faith not rationale to make sense. God, Heaven, an afterlife-none of the main concepts that the religious hold dear are rational or are "agreeable or in accord with reason." I wondered how so many people were content with irrational conclusions. How can they base something as important as their immortality on completely unsupported theory? Are they all just lazy, self-deluding, denial-loving nut jobs, or am I missing something?

For years I lived with the understanding that the belief in a God was a nonsensical, mythical delusion inspired by fear. At this point in my life, the "wise" and honest way to address life seemed to be from the posture of philosophical reasoning. Yet an important ingredient of that posture, which I feel many people overlook, is that the philosopher must also apply this beam of reasoning upon his or her assumptions and dogmatic views. You aren't quite true to the philosophical science if you are not willing to question your own relationship to philosophy or the philosophical science itself. If you aren't willing to do this, then you have only adopted a way of life in which to hide your fears, which is the very thing many philosophers spend their time criticizing the rest of the world for doing.

We all know people who "hide" from life in the intellect. These people will point a finger at "all the frightened, deluded [religious, materialistic, fanatical, etc.] people" as they slug back their martini, take another drag of their cigarette and file for another divorce, but they are lax at turning that same beam of criticism upon themselves. Not only do we need to question what we are doing in life but we must also question our motive for questioning what we decide to question and what we choose to overlook. Honesty with others is hard enough, but with ourselves, where nothing can hide from the observant, it is much harder.

Einstein once said:

We should take care not to make the intellect our god; it has, of course, powerful muscles, but no personality...Intelligence makes clear to us the interrelationship of means and ends. But mere thinking cannot give us a sense of the ultimate and fundamental ends. To make clear these fundamental ends and valuations and to set them fast in the emotional life of the individual, seems to me precisely the most important function which religion has to form in the social life of man.

Thinking Your Way There

Once there was a well-known philosopher and scholar who devoted himself to the study of Zen for many years. On the day that he finally attained enlightenment, he took all of his books out into the yard, and burned them all.

Unknown Author

CHAPTER FIVE

So, there I was minding my own business in lovely Boulder Colorado, going to my philosophy classes, smoking pot, and chasing women. Just like a good young-blooded American boy "should." Then one day I went home to find out that my mom went off to some spiritual conference, and she came back excited about spiritual crap. She was talking about how prayer, mantras, and *bhajans* can change the vibratory level of the body, mind, and spirit. How we have spiritual centers within the body called chakras. How we have been alive for thousands of years through reincarnation. The "law of karma" etc. etc. etc. I wasn't really listening to the details of what she was saying. I was more taken back by the degree of her passion for this new-found toy. It scared me. My mom hates religion as much as I do...who is this imposter?

I couldn't believe that my mother, who was my closest confidante in my fight against religious simplicity and my cohort in the champion of philosophical integrity, began associating with a religious organization. I was crushed. I was convinced she was brainwashed or that this time she actually did suffer a mental breakdown.

I thought, "How could she give up the fight to resist the evil empire of religion and the fear and judgment it preaches? This is not like her. She's too intelligent for this stuff. What could she see in it?" After six months of arguing with her I decided to check out what it was she was so excited about.

I have to admit I never would have stopped to check out religion at this point in my life if it wasn't for the deep respect I had for my mother. At this point in my life she was my closest friend and the only person I had found that I could call a mentor. I figured, "If it meant this much to her, then it might have some merit."

I went with her to a "spiritual retreat." Even though I was trying to be a good sport I still thought, "Oh no, a whole week with religious people. I'll go crazy." It was July 1988, and while my hippie, pot-smoking buddies were running off to some decadent jazz festival in New Orleans, I was going to Montana on a spiritual retreat with my mom...good grief.

So, the following week I drove to Montana. The ride itself was pretty amazing. Wyoming and Montana are incredibly beautiful states: mile after mile of rolling hills, rivers, mountains, and endless stretching skies. It was a very strange sight for a kid from New Jersey, America's most densely populated "Garden State."

After driving about half way across Montana we came to a little town called Livingston where we turned south on highway 89 and followed the Yellowstone River until we were literally in the middle of "Paradise Valley, Montana." Trust me, the valley is aptly named. The valley is lined with snowcapped mountains, which lurch thousands of feet upward towards the sky. The valley floor, several miles across, is lush with green rolling hills and groomed fields. There were horses and cattle sparsely scattered about and plenty of wildlife jetting across the highway. The life of the valley grows out from the Yellowstone River, which winds its way down the center of the valley. The blanket of greenery begins dark and rich on the river's edge and gradually blends through every shade of green until the fields reach the amber grasses at the mountains' edge. I have to admit my initial resistance towards spending the week with "wacky religious people" was becoming weaker.

The conference was held in a plush green meadow high up in the mountains on the southwest corner of Paradise Valley. The meadow was encircled with mountains with rocky pointed tips, which protruded well over the tree line. There was a creek, green grass, thickly packed pine trees, wildlife, and a gorgeous blue sky. This run-in with nature alone was a "moving" experience.

But even more surprising than the beautiful environment was the number of people and their attitude. To my surprise, over four thousand people descended on this valley from more than a dozen different countries. I met people from South Africa, Saudi Arabia, Brazil, Russia, Australia and numerous European countries. They brought their children, pitched tents, and were there to breathe in a great life-changing experience. Everyone was extremely friendly and excited as if some great event was about to take place.

It was pretty amazing to be around such a large crowd with such strong "other-worldly" aspirations. Some of the people were your typical weird, hippie, peace-loving kind of fake, new age whackos, but there was a startling number of very level-headed, well-educated people who seemed interested in having an intelligent conversation about life. Statistically this is an incredibly large number of levelheaded people for any setting I've ever attended. I met an ex-Christian minister, ex-Catholic nun, a college professor, a banker, a wealthy businessman, and many others who had bounced around from one religion or another because they claimed they weren't able find the spiritual experience they were looking for.

It was the first time in my life that I had met well-educated, levelheaded people who were interested in religion. To date, the only religious people I had known grazed at the altar like sheep. They didn't think. They didn't question. They did their Catholic calisthenics and went home and got drunk. To find intelligent people discussing and questioning religious concepts in a rational manner was quite a change. It was also strange to witness their determination. Many of these people traveled thousands of miles, packing along their kids, and were willing to camp out in the woods for a week in the rain and cold mountain air in hope of bringing away a little more understanding of why they were alive. I admired their conviction.

The average person I met in the world seemed to be oblivious to the fact that they did not know why they were alive. But now I was sitting up in the mountains with thousands of people who not only traveled very far physically to get here but many of them traveled very far emotionally and intellectually as well.

Many of the people I met could list numerous organizations, "teachings" or religious institutions they had associated with in the past. Not only had they attended many other religious or spiritual organizations but their participation in these organizations was rarely cursory. They would tell me how they spent years with this or that religion and intensely studied its text, debated its theories, rigorously participated in its rituals, took its teachings as far as they could, and then set out to find another teaching which could take them further.

Meeting and talking to these people was extremely interesting, but I must admit when it came time to actually sitting down with them and participating in "religious type stuff," I was very uncomfortable. The mountain meadow had several huge white tents, which could seat several thousand people in each one. They were doing eastern chants, *bhajans* (Hindi songs of prayer), western prayers; they were singing songs and listening to and giving lectures. I must admit it was a pretty awesome event to hear 4,000 people chanting the OM or AUM in this gorgeous mountain valley. Even for someone completely non-religious, as I was, it would be hard not to be moved by the power and beauty of the harmonious tone or the peace and tranquility upon the faces of thousands of people participating in it. I decided I would just sit and observe their rituals and listen to the lectures and prayers, but "Gosh darn it," my staunchly philosophical ego proclaimed, "I was not going to pray, and I wasn't going to sing any 'Kum ba yah' crap."

What also made the whole experience much easier for me was the fact that so much of the conference focused on eastern religious rituals and theology. At the time, although I was a dedicated philosopher, I was unaware, as I believed many were, that on occasion I had let the enemy of religion slip into my philosophical camp. In the 80s, many people I knew and who considered themselves to be strict "philosophers," would often read eastern religious writings without considering themselves violating the unwritten agreement to hate all religions. For some strange reason western religions were "clearly mythical silliness," but eastern religions were "cool."

So, without even realizing it, I had studied many "religious" concepts already. This unbeknownst intruder was the link that helped me forgive my mother for dragging "that thing," that religion, into our house. Having said this, it was still very hard for me to begin to listen to religious stuff at first. I wondered, "How could I benefit by believing in imaginary beings and, 'God' forbid, begin praying to these imaginary beings?"

I remember when I was a little kid and my grandmother took me to church and told me to go to confession. I asked, "What the hell for?" and she said, "For saying 'what the HELL for.'" So, I went into the booth, and I told the old man in the next box that I said the word HELL and he told me to go do five Hail Mary's and five Our Fathers. I hopped out of the box, walked over to a pew, rolled my eyes, and said ten times "This is stupid, this is stupid, this is stupid..." So not only did I not like religion for some time, but apparently, I was a brat as well.

So, the fact that the subject matter at the conference focused primarily on Eastern religions made it much easier for me to keep an open mind. What also made the religious event easier was the fact that when western religions were discussed, they were always arguing for interpretations contrary to the typical message I had heard from the average Christian or Jewish pulpit. I heard things like "Christ believed in the law of karma just like Buddha. Christ said, 'As you shall sow you shall also reap.' This is the law of karma. Christ was an ordinary man, who, through extraordinary effort, "woke up" to the realization that he, and we, had the power to become so much more. Christ taught that we could accomplish everything that he did. Why else would he say, "The works I do *ye shall do also and greater works* for I go unto my Father?'" (John 14:12) The Kabala teaches that God dwells within each person, and we are all capable of becoming one with God.

Christ, Buddha, and all the other founders of the great religions all taught that we are not the mere feeble, hapless, mortal beings destined to suffer from sadness, illness, disease, and death. That we can break free of this world's limitations completely just as Christ, Buddha, and many others have. That is

56

how the prophets embodied unconditional love, how they healed the sick, walked on water, and defied death.

[Let me interject here by saying that I am not endorsing this religion or any other particular religion. The place I am talking about in Paradise Valley, Montana is a pretty standard church now, and although it espouses many spiritual practices, its hierarchy preaches dogma and control of the experience. Some of their spiritual teachings are very extreme and distracting from what I feel is a simple path of self-understanding. Participating in any religion or organized gathering will be at your own peril. I could write volumes on the problems with the unenlightened interpreting spiritually for each other, but I'm sure you can surmise the obvious problems.]

As I listened to these lectures I began to hear a message of empowerment and not the typical "Jesus is the shepherd and you are dumb sheep." They were saying things like everyone can become enlightened. They believed that everyone could become liberated from the typical human condition of fear and selfishness. That everyone can do what Christ, Buddha, Lao Tzu, Krishna, Abraham, Mohammed and Mother Teresa did. That everyone can become just like them. These prophets were not special because who they were but because who they became. They believed that we were not sent here to worship the prophets but rather to emulate them. The prophets were not born as gods but rather they were just like us and then became these amazing beings through their hard work and realizations.

It was shocking for me to hear such a different and self-empowering interpretation of the religions. It was almost intimidating to contemplate that I could possibly become as peaceful and powerful as people like Christ, Buddha, or any of the various Jewish, Muslim, or Hindu Prophets. To embody such mastery as to actually break free from the confines of this world while still in the world. To be able to transcend suffering, to love without ever hating and to never fear. Is this possible?

Well, I must admit I never knew there was room within religion for such lofty conquests. I was shocked by the gall of these people to read into the religious text the ability of the common person to become an equal to Christ. Christ was supposed to be God's son, and we were the lowly sinners. How did we get promoted to have access to the first chair in the orchestra next to

God himself? Either these people were able to realize this because they were smarter and less fearful than the average person or they were egotistical maniacs spewing the worst blasphemies. Either way, I was kind of digging it. It, at the very least, deserved further investigation.

I began to wonder, is it really possible to tap into some consciousness that flowed through all things? Could I actually walk a path that would lead me to become such a powerful spiritual being? Why are there so many accounts of people like Buddha, Christ, Enoch, Lao Tzu, Gandhi, Rama Krishna, Mohammad, and hundreds of others who apparently tapped into some great knowledge while sitting silently in some corner of the world? Many men and women have accomplished this great task in every corner of the world while sitting in quiet contemplation. How is it that you can come upon wisdom while sitting in silent meditation? Where is this information coming from? Is there really some internal way of tapping into some great source of wisdom?

Remember, at this point in my life I was the philosopher who learns by gathering information from my five senses and then analyzing that information with the mental function of reason. To date, no philosopher I knew of had been able to figure out the purpose for human existence. There must be something missing in the typical application of gathering information via the five senses and analyzing it. I'm unaware of anyone who has succeeded in gathering the information necessary for the mind to understand the reason for our existence. Yet, the religions claim to have hundreds of people who have found the meaning of life.

At the time it seemed to me that these enlightened people weren't finding enlightenment through the outer senses but through some event that occurs in silence. Where were they getting this information? They claimed to have found it by turning away from the "distraction" of the senses and the outer world. They found it within. They claimed there was a better way of gathering information, and it was not from our outer sense but from some type of inner sense or senses.

"Man, therefore, looks outward," observes the Hindu text the Upanishads. "Man, therefore, looks toward what is outside, and sees not the inward being. Rare is the wise man who shuts his eyes to outward things and so beholds the glory or the Atman within."

Only that yogi
Whose joy is inward,
inward his peace,
And his vision inward
Shall come to Brahman
And know Nirvana.

(Bhagavad-Gita, Prabhavananda & Isherwood translation, Ch. V.)

Mahatma Gandhi put it so simply when he was asked how a person finds enlightenment. He responded by saying, "Turn the spotlight inward."

I began to consider that maybe I had not found the meaning of life because I was looking for it in the wrong place. Maybe, these religious people had found a way to gather more or different information for the mind to apply its reason to. Where were these guys going in their meditations? Were they actually tapping into a source of information, or were they simply creating more elaborate myths?

So what was I going to do? Do I try this path? Do I investigate? Should I give it a whirl? I sat there and looked at the statue of Buddha which was sitting in one of the corners of the tent, and I saw an expression of peace I had never seen on any successful business person nor on the face of the even the wittiest philosopher. So, I decided there was only one way to figure out if the spiritual path had anything to offer. I decided to try it.

Devotion

A martial arts student went to his teacher and said earnestly, "I am devoted to studying your martial system. How long will it take me to master it?"

The teacher's reply was casual, "Ten years."

Impatiently, the student answered, "But I want to master it faster than that. I will work very hard. I will practice every day, ten or more hours a day if I have to. How long will it take then?"

The teacher thought for a moment, "20 years."

Unknown Author

Humility

To a visitor who described himself as a seeker after truth the master said, "If what you seek is truth, there is one thing you must have above all else."

"I know. An overwhelming passion for it."

"No. An unremitting readiness to admit you may be wrong."

Teachings of Father Anthony DeMello

CHAPTER SIX

So, I decided to try the spiritual path. Once I got past the fear of my philosophical peer's criticism, I became excited about the new path and its prospects. I was so psyched to have finally found something to do with my life that seemed not only challenging but also endlessly rewarding. I no longer had to choose between a life of pursuing success and a life of playing the intellectual critic of the path of success. One road was a life of defending an illusion and the other was a life of criticizing an illusion. Neither gets you anywhere because no matter how hard you try to improve your existence in relation to an illusion, you are still working off of an unreality. It is difficult to get closer to understanding reality by attempting to improve or disprove an unreality.

I began to understand that the "spiritual path" is a path of striving towards a deeper wisdom about who we are and why we exist. It was not a path of hiding behind myths like many people view religion nor was it the dead-end path of the constant critic. Buddha and Christ and the other spiritual teachers seemed to be saying that the spiritual path is a path towards unlimited "growth." In addition, the only regulator of how far and fast a person could grow was based on the degree of their own determination. So far this sounded like a good deal to me. It was a path with endless creative possibilities and supposed limitless knowledge and bliss. What is not to like? So, I decided to set out and do whatever it was Christ and Buddha and all the rest did in order to reach that deep meditation that brought them such wisdom and peace.

So how did they accomplish this? How did they reach a state of great wisdom, great bliss? I began to read about the lives of Christ and Buddha and their teachings regarding the spiritual path, and my elation quickly turned to "What? Are they nuts?" The honeymoon ended quite abruptly. Apparently, Buddha literally walked around the forest of Northern India for years, practicing different forms of asceticism, which is a practice of abstaining from the normal pleasures and materialistic comforts of life. That's right *abstaining from pleasures and comforts*.

Apparently, Christ and all the other spiritual guys likewise practiced various degrees of asceticism. Prior to reaching deep spiritual meditation these spiritual teachers completely abstained from alcohol, sex, and drugs. They wandered around deserts and forest and starved themselves almost to death. What the hell were they thinking? I began to think, "Whoa, hold the presses. Just one minute."

After learning about this whole asceticism thing my elation and plans of becoming "a great spiritual being" quickly faded to "You've got to be kidding." No booze...I'm a warm-blooded Irish-American it's not possible. No sex...let's not even go there. No worldly distractions...I'll go completely nuts. This ascetic stuff may have been possible back in the day when there wasn't much to do once the sun went down, but since the advent of electricity nighttime is a little more exciting than in the BC days. With all our modern toys and avenues of escape it's simply too much to ask anyone–especially a twenty-one-year-old kid living in America, the land of opportunity for multiple forms of immediate gratification, to give it all up.

At first this spiritual stuff seemed to be a pretty good idea, but now I wasn't so sure. Most of the activities I came to rely upon in my life for pleasure, sex, drugs and booze, apparently are thought of as distracting activities to the spiritual student. There are few things more frightening than the thought of surrendering activities that are the main source of our pleasure.

Now you may be thinking, as I was, how in God's name could an activity, which brings such pleasure, be bad? Well, "bad" is probably not the right word. Buddha and Christ explain that in order to understand your attachment to these activities and the effect of your attachment to these activities it helps to "suspend" participation in them.

Part of the problem, they would say, is that if you are so used to finding a considerable degree of pleasure from the world around you, it will be hard to spend quality time concentrating and analyzing your attachments because soon after you sit down to meditate your mind wants to go out for a beer. In addition, as we will discuss in great detail, it is your attachments that are what keeps you from bliss and not the act itself. Booze, sex, and drugs are not "bad" nor the cause of our suffering. It is our attachment to them that does. If you want to escape fear and anxiety, you must be able to "break" your attachments. It is very hard to break an attachment if you believe you cannot experience pleasure without that activity.

I would like to share a deep secret about the spiritual path that nobody mentioned to me at the beginning and a secret I had to figure out on my own after being on the path for several years. You do not have to abstain from worldly pleasures forever. The truth is that after several years of abstention from worldly pleasures, the student can return to participation in these pleasures once again. The break from worldly pleasures is only temporary. So don't fret if a great sit-com comes out while you're off meditating. You can download those seasons later and get fully caught up. Or worse, don't resist the spiritual path because of your fear of losing pleasure. The spiritual path, it turns out, teaches us to enjoy pleasure so much more because we learn to do so without the negative side effect of the fear of losing it. I'll explain this in detail later.

Most teachers do not teach this "temporary suspension issue" at the beginning of the path. They are afraid their students will never truly be able to let go of these pleasures to the degree necessary to reach deep concentration if they are constantly thinking about the day they can return to their outer pleasures. Although I share their concern on this issue, I think it does more harm than good because too many students never enter the path at all since they fear the discomfort of abstaining from their pleasures for the rest of their life.

Some people, wrongly, avoid the spiritual path because they think it requires a dull life of constant meditation with no pleasure. The truth of the matter is the exact opposite. Imagine experiencing life with no fear of acceptance, regret, fear of loss, etc. I would rather see more people enter the spiritual path and then help them let go of destructive attachments (not actions) than to have them never attempt to understand this concept at all.

I do not think most people have been told that the different religions all explain the same path but from different perspectives. At this point in my journey, the perspective most attractive to me was Buddhism. Buddha's enlightenment resulted from the profound understanding of the source of all human suffering. Buddha, according to legend, was shocked unto the path of enlightenment out of a deeper than usual ignorance about life. Buddha's father was a king of sorts. He was very wealthy and out of love for his son he decided to raise young Siddhartha (Buddha's birth name) within the confines of the palace grounds so that Buddha would never know nor witness the harsh reality of life's sickness, decay, and death. No one sick, old, or dying was allowed to interact with the young prince.

When he was a young adult he ventured out into the surrounding village for the first time. He took four trips. On the first trip he saw an old man. The second trip he saw a sick person. On the third trip he saw a dead person. On the last trip it was a religious devotee. The effect of these experiences was obviously shocking and profound. Buddha, not knowing of suffering due to his father's protective upbringing, jumped directly from the innocence of a child to the harsh realities of adulthood without the typical gradual progression. In a way, he snapped. He learned of pain, decay, and loss all at the same time while simultaneously witnessing the religious man who seemed to be more at peace with reality than others. He ran off in the middle of the night and declared he would not stop searching until he found the end to all human suffering.

It is important to note that Buddha, Jesus, and most others that have become enlightened were not and never were "religious." In this sense I am defining "religious" as accepting and practicing dogmatic ritual or in any other way acting and thinking like your typical "religious" person. I realize that this statement will be highly unpopular, but it's true. Jesus strongly disliked the Pharisees and priests of his time. Read the Bible. He bitches about them constantly. As an example, in Matthew 23:13, Jesus says "But woe to you, scribes and Pharisees, hypocrites! Because ye shut up the kingdom of heaven against men: for ye go not in, nor suffer those who are entering to go in."

Buddha, although he seems to show less disdain than Jesus for the religious, never was nor ever became "religious" even though he found enlightenment. Jesus found "God" but not due to his adherence to any particular religion but rather through his enlightenment and not the other way around. Both men found enlightenment due to their will and ability to observe what and who was ailing their own psychology. They were both philosophers who applied their determined reason upon themselves. Instead of the typical philosopher that loves to apply her reasoning outward upon the world, these guys did the same

71

THE MEANING OF LIFE: ONE MAN'S JOURNEY AND DISCOVERY OF LIFE'S MOST IMPORTANT QUESTION

thing but upon themselves. They discovered not only what made them unhappy but also the cause of all human unhappiness and the remedy. That was it. Plain and simple.

Buddha, through many years of meditation and asceticism, realized that our fundamental misunderstanding of the source of "happiness" causes all sorrow. Ironically, Buddha realized that it is the way we pursue happiness which actually causes our unhappiness. Buddha realized that humans are unwittingly trapped in a cycle of unhappiness. Somehow, we have come to believe that our happiness, naturally, will always be coupled with a degree of anxiety. Buddha's great awakening, the word Buddha means "Awoken One" in Hindi, made him realize that humans could move beyond this happiness/anxiety-entwined experience. This blissful state is called Nirvana.

So, what does Buddha mean when he says that we are all experiencing happiness coupled with anxiety? This, in my opinion, is the most profound realization ever discovered regarding the human condition. It is so simple that it is hard to grasp. Likewise, we are so accustomed and enmeshed with our present understanding of happiness that it is hard to step outside of it in order to look back and analyze it. Let me try to describe the typical perspective on happiness and try to help you see what Buddha saw.

Our current understanding of happiness is that it comes from a process of *desiring* an experience and then trying to *satisfy* that desire by causing that experience to occur. Let us break that process down. A person decides that if a particular event occurred in their life then that occurrence would make them happy. In other words, the process begins when we desire something. This occurrence could be any number of things or experiences.

As you can imagine the list of things a person could desire is almost endless. On any given day the average person is desiring dozens of things to occur in his or her life: a new job, more money, a romantic partner, a house, a car, an education, a fun trip, food, games, mindless entertainment, thoughtful entertainment, sex, to be thinner, to have more hair, to be less hairy, to be liked, to do something good for others, to be admired, to feel confident, to no longer worry, to feel whole, to be secure financially, personally and professionally, to be healthy, to have a purpose, to have a job that is more creative, to have a spouse who

73

is more understanding, to have loving children, to have loving parents, to be paid attention to, to have caring friends, to feel happy, to be feared, to be idolized, to be powerful, to be respected, to be admired, to be liked, to be a better person, to know the meaning of life etc. The list can go on practically forever.

For most of us we can relate to the standard template of "we want to get into a good college so we can get a high paying job so we can attract that good-looking spouse and be able to buy the nice house and car and have the two children and a dog and never have to worry about bills so we can go on nice trips and be viewed by our peers as someone who is successful." Yikes...are we that predictable? Pretty much.

So we all have our lists of desires. Now we must spend our life trying to acquire that which we desire. Buddha realized that people around the world were suffering from the anxiety caused by their desire for things and events to occur in their life. All people are in a state of "I'll be happy someday once the things I desire come to fruition." This is quite a revelation that the entire world is only experiencing the anticipating of happiness and not happiness in the present sense. We have all set up conditions that must be satisfied for our happiness to occur.

Once we believe that we need this desire fulfilled for us to feel happy, then our happiness is contingent upon us actually satisfying it. So, off we go into life in pursuit of the fulfillment of all of our dreams. Suffering, as Buddha defines it, is the anxiety that builds due to our stress of trying to acquire those things and events. As you can imagine, the list above takes time to acquire. If our complete happiness will remain on hold until all is obtained, then we consign ourselves to many years of enjoying little successes or failures in pursuit of our goals. But, ultimately, complete happiness is suspended until some distant future because we will always have a list of things we still "desire."

Rarely does life work out the way we intended. Upon each "failure" or change in our future we must make a new list of how we want life to unfold. This can be brought about by never getting that degree, marrying the wrong person or being the wrong person for a happy marriage, not being able to have kids, realizing you will never be rich etc., etc, etc. Many people are living a life of "compromised" desires and reevaluated future ones. I, as an example, never did become that astronaut I envisioned, but I was a cab driver, so I, too, have made some adjustments.

If I haven't made you completely depressed, hang on, it gets worse. Get this: even if we are lucky enough to obtain one of the things we always wanted, then comes the fear of losing it. For the love of God, can we get a break? This entire process sucks!

The entire process is not black and white either. We are constantly renegotiating with life and sliding back and forth along a scale of satisfaction. Even while we are satisfying some of our desires, there are always other desires which are not yet satisfied and many of them fall into different categories of likely to get satisfied, may get satisfied, and probably won't get satisfied.

So even when some of our dreams are finding satisfaction, we are never experiencing complete peace because there are many other desires still waiting to be satisfied. Then there is the whole realm of partially satisfied desires: "I have a job that pays ok, but it isn't that satisfying"; "we have a house but I would like a nicer one in a better part of town"; "I have a marriage but it needs a lot of work, etc." There is very little peace in this process. We are always in a state of wanting.

One of the main problems with this process is that our minds are infinitely thinking up better ways of finding happiness. We constantly want new and better things. Our relationships can always be improved. Our work could always be less stressful or more interesting. Our social life could be more exciting. We could always be more successful. We wish we could reduce the unhappiness of people we care about. We wish we had more money so we could fix up this house, buy a house, give our kids a better education, take our family on nice trips, buy a new car, work less and have more fun. The list never ends. The more and more money we make the more and more we find new things that we need. This doesn't even include the emotional experience of people who are well below poverty. Some desperately believe if they just had money all their troubles would be gone and some have given up hope for happiness because they now think the things they "need" are fatally beyond reach.

The wealthy don't fare any better. They suffer from an equally long list of things they need before they will be happy or obstacles to their happiness: the fear of losing all the wealth they have come to rely on, jealousy, pride, wanting a loving spouse and loving well-adjusted children, desiring acquaintances that like me and not my money, seeking acceptance and respect etc. etc. etc.

Another major problem with the way we pursue happiness is that it automatically causes pain to those around us. In other words, our search for happiness is actually the cause of almost all human violence. You may be asking, "How this could be?" Well, there is a limited supply of things in the world that everybody wants. There are limited high paying jobs, beautiful and kind spouses, houses by the sea, etc. Therefore, for us to get all the things we believe we need to be happy, we must outperform those around us. Every time we "succeed" at gathering what we feel we need, there is less for others to find. All the world is pitted against each other in a mad dash for the goods that bring happiness. And the winners ride around in their trophies, flaunting it at those who go without. Some people will harbor gross excess even while there are millions of starving, suffering children.

Most of the world will not get a good education, a high paying job, a nice house; many will never find love, have a family, or enjoy nice vacations. So, our understanding of happiness comes at a great price, and that price is the unhappiness of others. But, to understand this concept, you must understand that under this process nobody wins, not even those who become wonderfully adept at gathering the experiences they desire. They may experience many moments of pleasure coupled with anxiety, but they will never have true peace of mind. Through this process they will never experience the never ending and unconditional joy and peace of Nirvana. No one will ever experience true peace as long as they believe that these experiences/things/people are the source of their happiness. The angst of acquiring or the fear of losing will always live just below the surface. Wanting can never equate to peace. It will always be a state of yearning, wanting, and hoping for happiness. Peace or true happiness is something different.

Buddha's entire mission was to help people understand that this process is the cause of our suffering. He once said, "I did not create a religion but rather I found a way to escape suffering." Buddha realized that if we could cease our endless desiring we could likewise end our endless anxiety. We are all living a life trying to quench a thirst that will never be satisfied.

I had read Buddha's *Four Noble Truths* a hundred times over fifteen years before I began to truly understand them. It reads: All the world is suffering, all the world is suffering due to desire, the way to escape this suffering is to become selfless, and the way to become selfless is through the Eightfold Path. What I have been discussing above is the first two "Truths." Simply put, all the world is suffering due to desire. It took me fifteen years to figure out the depth and the everyday practical application of what he was saying, but when it hit me, I realized the irony is our pursuit of happiness causes unhappiness.

We have been taught a flawed system of finding happiness, and this flawed system is the cause of our suffering.

Awareness

"I laughed when they told me that the fish in the water was thirsty."

Kabir, The Kabir book: Forty-four of the ecstatic poems of Kabir

CHAPTER SEVEN

Although the concept of abstaining from worldly pleasures began to make more sense to me, it didn't seem to make the prospect that much more inviting. I hung around the conference site in Montana for another week, meeting people and trying to convince myself that I could actually try to live this life. At one point, I was sitting in one of the huge tents at a long picnic table having lunch with my mom. I was bitching and complaining to her about the concept of abstaining from "wine, women and song" when some guy sat down across the table from us. I was saying, "Why couldn't I find this path when I was forty or fifty years old? Why couldn't I have found this path after I had more time to play? I'm only twenty-one years old. Think of all the fun I'm gonna miss if I give up drinking and playing now. I'm too young; I can't do it."

The guy across the table quickly dropped his fork in his brown rice and leaned forward as if he just *had* to say something.

"Excuse me for butt'n in," he said in a deep New York accent, "but I heard what you just said about wishing you found your spiritual path when you were forty or fifty years old...and...I need to tell ya...I mean...well..." He was really worked up over something. "I'm forty-four years old, and, God damn it, I would have given my right arm to have found this path when I was your age. Why do you want to live another day let alone another twenty-five years in the dark? If I could only tell you all the stupid shit I've done over the last twenty-five years and all the people I've hurt in the process. You know over the last twenty-five years not a single day passed that I didn't think to myself, 'Please, God, give me a sign, show me there is a purpose to this crazy life, help me find a life worth living.' You should be so grateful that you found a path worth walking at such an early age. It is such an opportunity." Although I didn't want to hear it, on some level, I knew this guy was right.

For the next couple of days I walked around the conference site in a daze. There was an all-out war going on inside of me. Think about it. Imagine right now if you were considering quitting your job or school and joining a convent or monastery and agreeing to an indefinite term of celibacy, sobriety, and all-out abstention from all other worldly comforts. You would be a bit preoccupied as well.

I'm still not sure if there is a devil but I'm pretty sure he and I had a few words over the next couple of days. As I wandered around in my trance, I was pulled between the imploring of the little angel on my right shoulder saying, "Come on, this is exactly what you have been waiting for. It's a road of unlimited opportunity to grow and see what you can become. This is the path that all the great spiritual masters have walked. This is the life of meaning and purpose you have been looking for."

On the other shoulder was a huge red dude with a tail and horns. He had a mug of beer in one hand and a half dozen chicks in bikinis dancing around him and he was saying, "*WHAT ARE YOU F#*&ING THINKING???* Come on man, this is nuts. This is nothing but a crazy cult. Get your ass out of here and back to Boulder where the chicks run braless, the drugs are plentiful, and the world is your oyster. Come on, check out these hot young Betties. Are you really going to go without any nookie for the rest of your life? Who are you kidding? There's time to do this shit later in life. Go explore the world first. This place will always be here. Have a little fun before you buckle down."

It was the most tormenting three days of my life. All hell broke loose inside of me during that time. It may be the most difficult decision a person can ever make. It was for me. I came so close to saying the hell with this crap. I'm going back to school and I'll look this place up again in twenty years.

The last day of the conference I did something I've never done before. I walked into the main tent where they were holding the religious services. It was practically empty except for a few stragglers sitting around looking all pious. I walked up towards the front of the tent where there was an altar, I sat in a chair, and I began to talk to, I don't know who, I guess...God. I didn't know who or what the heck God was, but if there was a force that helps people walk the spiritual path then I was calling to it. I was not praying. I was outright begging for the strength to take the first step down this path. "Please, please God if you exist, then please help me. Please give me the strength to do this. I beg you. Give me the strength to break free from the ties to this world and to its toys and pleasures. Please God help me see what the path has to offer. Help me drown out my attachment to desire as my only source of pleasure and help me find a greater peace."

I sat there for at least an hour or more. Actually I have no idea how long I was there. But something happened to me during that time. My fear seemed to vanish. I began to feel excited. I began to feel like I was about to begin an amazing journey. I stood up from that seat with the full conviction to begin my spiritual journey. I walked out of that tent, and I knew they were my first steps on "The Path" and that from that moment forward there would be nothing ordinary about my life.

Knowing and Being

DISCIPLE: What's the difference between knowledge and enlightenment?

MASTER: When you have knowledge, you use a torch to show the way. When you are enlightened, you become a torch.

Teachings of Father Anthony DeMello

CHAPTER EIGHT

Most of us know someone who decided one day to "become religious." You could see them from a mile away. They would have that deranged, over-enthusiastic smile permanently painted on their face with that glazed, brainwashed look in their eyes. They were so annoying with their constant reference to "their lord and savior," "all glory to God," "praise the Lord," "born again," or being "saved." The whole time you are talking to them you can feel them trying to wrestle the conversation towards proselytizing. And, of course, we cannot forget their annoying condemnation towards "them sinners," which, of course, includes you. As Jesus warned us in Matthew 6:1 "Beware of practicing your righteousness before other people in order to be seen by them, for then you will have no reward from your Father who is in heaven."

Religious conversions typically happen to people who are experiencing a significant degree of fear due to some uncertainty about their life. It could be a time when a close loved one died, they are threatened with severe financial, professional, personal difficulties, or with any number of challenging events which can cause a person to experience extreme discomfort or confrontation with the uncertainty of life or death. In order to combat these fears these people find a belief system that soothes these fears, and they call it "religion."

If it is death you fear, "then don't fret because if you simply believe in Jesus Christ as your lord and savior, when you die an angel will appear to you, attach wings on your back so you can fly, give you very comfy sandals and a white robe, and you will sleep on clouds while the majority of the world who are Buddhist, Hindus, Jews and Muslims, Atheist, undecided or other will rot in a fiery hell for eternity." Religion has become the one stop mini mall of fear pacification. Name what you are afraid of and, "Jesus Christ shall save you from all calamity."

With religion, there is no need to take responsibility for your life and the choices you have made in order to create the life you are currently experiencing. Remember, you are not responsible because "you could not help yourself because you are only human, born with sin. But that's okay because Jesus Christ has already forgiven you and will save you regardless of what hideous things you have done to others...simply believe." This is what I call fast food salvation. This guaranteed instant salvation has absolutely no Biblical support. But, there will always be people who will believe it because it feels good and is easy.

Let me give you an easy litmus test to help you to spot those who have had a "religious conversion" versus a more thoughtful conversion, which I am encouraging. The person who had the religious conversion will believe that they now belong to an elite group of people, sometimes referred to as the "chosen ones," and they are now one of the few who will be saved at life's end due to the fact they share this one "true" theology. The billions of people who "fail" to call God by the same name as these people or who "fail" to proclaim their salvation by the same string of words as they do will, of course, be damned to an eternity of pain and misery.

The person who has experienced the spiritual conversion will not be tempted by such egocentric illusions of grandeur. Rather, they will realize the truth: all people are equal in God's eyes regardless of their belief system. God doesn't give a crap whose name you use but rather how selfless you are. How pure is your love for yourself and one another? As Christ said, "Not everyone that saith unto me, Lord, Lord, shall enter into the kingdom of heaven; but he that doeth the will of my Father which is in heaven. Many will say to me in that day Lord, Lord, have we not prophesied in thy *name*? and in thy *name* have cast out devils? and in thy *name* done many wonderful works? And then will I profess unto them, I never *knew* you: depart from me, ye that work iniquity" (emphasis added, Matthew 7:21-23).

In Christ's own words he said, I don't give a crap whose name you use. Words don't get you to heaven but they that "do" the will of God. Christ warned us to be aware of these idiots who come claiming to be enlightened in his name. Christ said, "Beware of the false prophets, which come to you in sheep's clothing, but inwardly they are ravening wolves. Ye shall know them by their fruits" (Matthew 7:15-16). What Christ meant is that you will know the quality of their intentions or level of enlightenment by what they "do" not what they say.

Religion was never intended to be about pacifying fear or about creating an "us" versus "them" mentality amongst people. Religion has been hijacked by the fearful and turned into a platform of hatred, power, and delusion. The prophets who started the various religions preached the exact opposite. Religion is not meant to be a series of concepts to hide from your fears. It should be a vehicle in which to confront your fears and overcome them.

Lift the Eyelid and the Result is Sight

"May I become your disciple?"

"You are only a disciple because your eyes are closed. The day you open them you will see there is nothing you can learn from me or anyone."

"What then is a Master for?"

"To make you see the uselessness of having one."

Teaching of Father Anthony DeMello

Be in Heaven

To a disciple who was obsessed with the thought of life after death the master said, "Why waste a single moment thinking of the hereafter?"

"But is it possible not to?"

"Yes."

"How?"

"By living in heaven here and now."

"And where is this heaven?"

"In the here and now."

Teachings of Father Anthony DeMello

CHAPTER NINE

I woke up on the last day of the conference, and I was feeling a bit uneasy. As I made my way up to the conference site I realized my anxiety was coming from the prospect of heading back to Colorado and somehow keeping the motivation to pursue the spiritual path. Although trying to overcome my attachment to desires made complete sense to me at the moment, I wasn't that confident it would make as much sense a few weeks later while strolling across campus and the laughter coming from the beer gardens and the sorority girls playing volleyball in their bikinis. I had a sneaking suspicion I just might slowly drift back to a life of playing before I knew it. If the little devil on my shoulder was able to rattle my cage this effectively up here in the mountains, I could only imagine the noise he could make once I returned to campus. So what was I going to do?

I was playing hacky sack with my brother and a few of the younger guys when some lady walked up and asked us if any of us would be interested in sticking around the conference site for a few days after the conference end to help take down tents and clean up. As payment they would provide housing, food, and reimburse our conference fees. Instantly, this sounded like a perfect way to postpone the inevitable. I began to think, "Yeah, I'll just hang around and do odd jobs for, let's say, the next twenty or thirty years, and I'll never have to worry about going back to the temptation of life. What a great idea." I quickly signed up and acted as if I was such a nice guy for volunteering to stay around and help out when, in fact, I was grateful they were willing to feed me while I hid from life.

The next day while the crowds were packing up and heading home I joined up with a group of guys who worked for the Church that conducted the conference. As we were pulling down tents they began to explain to me the structure of their church. Approximately 700 people lived there in Montana on 33,000 pristine acres, which encompassed several mountain peaks and ran down to the center of Paradise Valley to the Yellowstone River. In addition to the people at the ranch there were thousands of other members around the world. Their religion encompassed the teachings and practices of almost all the major religions.

Although they focused primarily upon Buddhism, Christianity, Hinduism, and Judaism, they often reference Islam, Sufism, Taoism, Zoroastrianism, and Confucianism.

The 700 people who lived on the ranch were given room and board and a very small stipend each month. The ranch was almost a self-sufficient community. They had doctors, nurses, chiropractors, and a variety of other health practitioners. The kitchen would serve three buffet meals to all 700 people 7 days a week. They grew a lot of their own food using organic farming methods. They did everything but make their own clothes. They had a school for the children and a three-month intensive course for people from off the commune to come and study their theology.

After working quietly and listening to these guys trying their best to sell me their organization, I was thinking to myself, "My, what a lovely cult you have here." I mean, everyone was really nice and actually quite intelligent, but come on, this place had "crazy cult" written all over it. It's not like I thought my life was in danger, but let me put it this way, I did make a point not to drink the colorful juice in the big bowl in the cafeteria. But, being of the adventurous spirit, I figured it wouldn't hurt to hang out for a week or two, enjoy the free food and the pure wackiness of hanging out at a cult for a few weeks. How many people get to say that they hung out in a cult for a couple of weeks? I thought it would make for an interesting story.

During the two weeks I spent a lot of time hiking in the mountains and thinking about what my life would look like when I returned to Colorado. I really wanted to give the spiritual path a try, but I couldn't see pulling it off back at the University of Colorado. It was 1988, I was twenty-one years old and had quite the thirst for booze, girls, drugs and fun. I simply didn't have the discipline to forgo these distractions when confronted by them. Oh, I think I failed to mention that at the time I was living with nine girls and two guys in a house just off campus about one block from the main strip of bars. I highly doubt I was going to meditate much in that atmosphere.

So what were my options? As the time passed I began to realize why these crazy cult people moved to Montana. It is much easier to concentrate when you don't have all the noise and distraction of the city in your face twenty-four hours a day. Up here there was no television, no billboards, no noisy streets, sirens, drugs, bikinis, or booze. It began to make sense to me why the gurus of India brought their students up to the mountains to study. The weak minded are easily distracted. Therefore, it is easier to concentrate if you remove the distraction.

But I lived in the land of distraction. I actually worked hard at arranging my life so that it would have tons of distraction right at my fingertips. You don't rent a house with nine girls between the ages of nineteen to twenty-two a half block from the bars because you are a recluse. You do it because at the time it wasn't thought of as distraction but rather considered a blast. To the average twenty-one-year-old kid, I planned my life quite perfectly.

But I had to think fast. My two weeks on the cleanup crew were coming to an end, and soon I would be out of my free mountainous room and board. I think I was the first person ever worried about being kicked out of a cult. I wasn't ready to leave, so I inquired about hanging around for a while. Guess what they said...they didn't have room. I couldn't believe it. I was rejected by a crazy cult. What are the chances of that? I mean, who gets thrown out of a cult? What kind of crazy psycho did they think I was? I was like, "You've got to be kidding me. Aren't you supposed to be trying to brainwash me into thinking that I couldn't live without this place?" But they were like, "Thanks for your help. Have a nice day" Shit, I'm cultless.

The only thing they could offer was that I could come back for a three-month class in the fall. It started in about eight weeks. It was a twelve-week course that covered a basic review of all the major religions and a basic understanding of how to reach deep meditation. So, I signed up.

But what was I going to do with myself for the next eight weeks? It had now been three weeks and I hadn't had any booze or smoked any dope. This was the longest I had gone completely sober since I began partying in my early teens. I figured I had a better chance of making it back in the fall if I stayed sober for the rest of the summer than if I began to party again and try to quit all over again.

So, that was my game plan. I would go back to Boulder, give up my apartment, move my stuff to storage for a couple of months, and try to avoid partying. I drove off from the ranch with a knot in my stomach, but I was determined to make it back to Montana for the class in the fall. I was afraid that after a couple of months I would slowly start forgetting the beauty I felt while up in the mountains and that look of peace on Buddha's face.

All the way back to Boulder I kept repeating Buddha's noble truths:

All the world is suffering
and all the world is suffering due to desire
and the way to stop suffering is to become desireless.

I got back to Boulder around midnight on a Tuesday, and, of course, there was a full-on raging party going on in the house. I tried to retreat to my room, but there was some guy already passed out in my bed and drooling on my pillow. I hung out for a while and tried to make small talk with some of my roommates, but after a while I just went out to the park across the street, laid on a bench, and wondered what the hell am I doing with my life?

The next day I rented a U-Haul, moved all my stuff to storage, and decided to take off to New Jersey for the summer. I thought if I am going to try to be a sober weirdo for the summer it would be easier to accomplish this around some of my buddies I grew up with. So, I showed up in Jersey and, in truth, it wasn't much easier there either. Partiers don't like it when their friends quit partying. It annoys them. They constantly want to know "what's wrong with having a few beers once in a while" or they will say "smoking pot is a very spiritual experience. I always feel more creative when I'm stoned." They constantly feel like you're judging them. I didn't give a crap if they wanted to get high, I just didn't want to get high with them. They instantly saw this as me judging them. I eventually stopped hanging out with them as well.

Even my closest friends with whom I have had hundreds of conversations regarding "finding the meaning of life" or "what is life all about" were annoyed with me, and every time I tried to talk to them about the experience I had in Montana, they would soon be back to saying "but what's wrong with getting stoned once in a while or having a few beers after work?"

And again I would find myself saying, "Nothing. I just want to try this path of learning to meditate to see what's out there. I'm told that in order to experience a real profound wisdom you must learn to still your mind completely, and apparently it is harder to do when your body is craving things from the world around you. So, I'm just going to go try it for a little while. Please don't take it personally."

One day I stopped by my grandmother's house and I began to tell her how hard it was on me that my friends were beginning to distance themselves from me. She was a 4'11" devout Catholic who emigrated from Ireland, and she had the most incredibly peaceful presence. We were sitting there having tea and Irish soda bread, and she looked at me and said, "It only takes one saint to make a house full of martyrs." She continued as she rose to get more tea. "You have to understand that the saints have always been rejected by the world. As soon as you try to improve yourself you will become a thorn in the side of anyone who is trying to run from life and its constant call for us to improve ourselves. Have you ever heard that misery loves company? Well, people are lazy and they will reject those who won't be lazy with them. They will criticize all those who try to break out and do something different. By not drinking, if you intend it or not, you are forcing everyone around you to question why they drink. They reject you because they are annoyed that you made them think. They don't want to think. They just want to get drunk. They want to go back to sleep. They don't want to go through the work it takes to question if there is a better way to live. I know it is hard, but simply ignore them. I think it is great that you are interested in religion." But then she threw in her Catholic pitch when she said, "But, why that place in Montana? It sounds like a cult. You can find everything you need in the Catholic Church. Whatever happens, if you *do* go back to Montana, please be careful." She was an amazing, sweet woman.

Scorn

A novice once went to Abbot Macario to ask his advice on how best to please the Lord. 'Go to the cemetery and insult the dead,' said Macario.

The brother did as he was told. The following day, he went back to Macario. 'Did they respond?' asked the Abbot.

'No,' said the novice.

'Then go and praise them instead.'

The novice obeyed. That same afternoon, he went back to the Abbot, who again asked if the dead had responded.

'No, they didn't,' said the novice.

'In order to please the Lord, do exactly as they did,' Macario told him.

'Take no notice of men's scorn or of their praise; in that way, you will be able to build your own path.'

Unknown Author

CHAPTER TEN

My foray onto the religious or spiritual path was, in hindsight, predominantly an egotistic endeavor. While there were many innocent and genuine ideas of becoming wiser and finding out the meaning of life, the true drive and vigor was caused by my ego's illusions of grandeur. Actually, I'm not sure anyone starts his or her path in any other way. I'm not sure we are capable of anything but an egotistic act because we are our ego. It effects *all* decisions. I know that this statement will not be received well, but it is very important for us to recognize the depth and breadth of the ego's control over our every thought. If we don't realize this, we will let it escape full prosecution or observation. This is extremely dangerous because the entire path to enlightenment is about understanding our relationship to the ego. If we fall into the dangerous mentality of "now I'm being egotistic" or worse, "now I'm being non-egotistic," we may believe there are times our ego is not affecting our thoughts/actions. Ask yourself, "Have I ever felt *proud* of myself because I did something good?" That is the ego applauding itself. You must assume, at all times, that your ego is calling the shots. If you assume otherwise, you are only being fooled by the ego.

One of my most powerful lessons of self-observation came during a weeklong "voice fast." For one week I did not speak. It was an amazingly difficult thing to do. It requires some understanding from family and friends. For strangers you just motion to your throat as if there is something wrong and you can't talk, and they will be happy to keep talking without your input. Try it for a few days, a week, or a year. Pythagoras used to require all his students to remain silent for three years prior to entering his school. It is an amazing tool of self-discovery. What I found was that it killed me not to join in the conversation. My petty little ego wanted to be heard. Every time I wanted to join in the conversation I had to stop myself, and then I would pay attention to what I wanted to say and why. It is astounding what you will learn. I eventually realized that everything I wanted to say was motivated to satisfy one of my ego's many "needs." I was listening to the others only to hear how I could get out of them what I wanted. What I wanted to say revealed what I actually wanted of them. Originally I thought I engaged with them because I enjoyed their company. In the end I realized that I engaged with them because I wanted their approval, their admiration, their respect, their companionship, and of some of them I wanted their physical comfort. There were many things that I wanted of them, and everything I wanted to say was calculated at acquiring one of my "needs" and likewise for them. If you realize what is going on between all of us, it is kind of crazy. There was very little room for anything resembling a selfless feeling or intention. I couldn't find one. I was way too busy trying to get the grocery list of things I wanted from people.

I believe that constructive self-observation requires a healthy degree of schizophrenia...if that's possible. Here is a warning. If you already have a problem with many confusing personalities, this technique may make matters worse. I really can't think of any other way to allow yourself to become detached or objective enough to observe what you are saying so you can learn who you are and what stupid things you are capable of. I found it liberating because when I was observing all the stupid childish stuff I wanted, I was somewhat removed from that stupid kid. I become the psychologist in the next room, the sociologist

107

on the street corner, and the academic at the back of the class. I became grateful not to be the child acting like an ass even though that child was me, even though that bully was me, even though that brat was me, even though that manipulator was me, even though that liar was me. I was simply observing.

I believe you must gain this ability to detach yourself; otherwise, you will be too eager to defend or justify your intentions because you are too close to feeling and fearing your desires not being realized. You have to be able to allow that personality or that need in you to fully express itself without you running back in to argue with it or justify it. Simply observe. You have to sit back and allow it to expose itself, and then you can come to understand it.

Man, know thyself. This process of self-observation is the process of knowing thyself. A voice fast is an extreme way to gain observation, but I was extremely ignorant of who I was. I needed it. And, once again, I'm not saying you need to do it. I'm just saying it worked for me. It started my practice of self-observance, which was the key to learning about myself and seeing the many personalities I had created over the years to service the many desires I had.

If we don't stay on top of it, the ego will hide and thereby continue its existence where you refuse to believe it exist. Don't be fooled that you are only acting egotistical when you are comparing yourself to others in competition or some other obvious "egotistical act." Until you are fully liberated from the ego like Buddha or Christ, there is no act, thought, or desire without the ego's input. You are the ego, and it is you. You are not in control of it. It and you are so intertwined that you can't see it because it is the one looking for itself. Do you think it wants to find itself and destroy itself?

For us to have this discussion I guess I should better define what we are discussing so we can be sure we are on the same page. For argument's sake let's assume that in each one of us there are two beings. You have "self" (some call it the "I" or the "soul") and you have the "ego." I realize that the word ego is a Latin word for "I," but believing that the ego is "you" or your true being, "self," is the main obstacle to enlightenment. I will explain that in detail later, but for now we need to define these words so we know what we are discussing. You don't need to agree with my definitions or descriptions of these aspects of self, but let's just use them for now to facilitate the discussion.

Freud went further and broke down the ego into three parts: the id (instinctual drives), super-ego (critical and moralizing role) and the ego (the realistic consciousness) that mediates between the base desires of the id and the idealism of the super-ego. I believe that Freud is missing the most important actor, which is the "self," which is our "true" self which can exist separately from the ego. This is evidenced by the fact that aspects of the ego are discarded constantly, and when that occurs we don't die. The self continues to exist. The ego we had as a teenager may be completely different than the one we have as an adult, yet we still consider "me" to be "me." The ego is an adaptable projection of the self and therefore not fundamentally the self. There must be something that continues while the ego is constantly discarded and rebuilt. I'll develop this theory more in a bit, but for now, when I use the word "ego," know that I am discussing all of the temporary personality traits that the self is projecting. Realize that this is done both consciously and unconsciously. We are sometimes aware that we are "acting

110

egotistical," and other times we believe that the projection is truly us and therefore an unconscious association to that persona.

We have spent our entire lives creating and layering our mind with various egotistical personalities which we believed we needed in order to address the various duties life has to offer (career ego, romantic ego, social ego, etc.). Then we eventually become the ego that is the orchestra leader of all the egos. Remember this entire process was started and encouraged at birth. By the time we were old enough to question the process, we are now questioning the existence of our ego with our ego. Don't fool yourself for a moment and think that you are free to observe your ego. You aren't. You must understand this in order to get past it. If you think your ego isn't manipulating the way you are observing yourself or anything else, then you are deluded. You must realize that you no longer have clear vision. You are wearing the glasses of your self-serving ego, which does not want to change, be analyzed, criticized, or discarded.

Your ego looks at everything through the lens of: how will this make me appear stronger, smarter, more attractive, give me a social edge, get me the pleasure I seek, make me someone to be admired, etc.! You cannot view anything without that lens. It took me twelve years to have my first experience where I felt I floated separate from the thoughts of my ego. It didn't mean that I had no ego. Oh, God no! I have an extremely vibrant ego, but I have learned to be able to step away from it on occasion and be an observer of its childish tirades. It has definitely lessened its obnoxiousness over the years, but it is still there all the time. You don't have to fight it. You can walk away, and I am learning to slowly walk away from my ego like gradually cutting ties with a destructive friend.

The important day is when you realize, "I am incapable of knowing when I am acting and when it is my ego, and therefore I must observe my thoughts constantly until I learn to recognize the fullness of my ego and its many personalities." Soon you will begin to see patterns in its childish reaction to similar social situations, and if you can observe yourself without arguing with your ego's attempt to defend that view or justify that position, you may be able to begin to see its outline. Your silent and internal ability to do this will be mirrored by your external fighting with others. How defensive are you when criticized by others? If you are quick to defend yourself, you are fully submerged in your ego, and you have little or no control over your thoughts and reaction in that situation. If you have the ability to pause and reflect and then think of a creative way to defend yourself, you simply have a more sophisticated ego.

If you are able to pause, analyze the criticism and actually find fault in yourself, then you are beginning to be able to analyze the ego, and you are on the path towards identifying and being able to quarantine this hideous virus. But never be fooled. I have seen my ego figure this out and pretend to pause, pretend to objectively analyze the criticism, pretend to make an adjustment. Then when I walked away, I realized I was proud of how incredibly mature I was becoming, which, of course, is 100% ego just pretending I've somehow changed.

If you come to me and tell me what a stupid book I wrote, or you say what a brilliant book I wrote and I let it affect me, if I react, there is the ego. The "soul" or whatever you want to call the person behind all the personalities doesn't give a rat's ass about your insult or compliment either way. That person just loves. It doesn't get hurt by criticism, nor does it become proud of praise. It cares only to the degree where it can learn and improve itself. It is impermeable to praise or criticism since it can't be hurt or elated.

You might be saying, "Well, this isn't human. It's robotic." You couldn't be more wrong. That person is liberated. That person's happiness is not precariously at the whim of the world's approval or disapproval. That person has the ability to be happy, truly happy, and to fully laugh, to truly love, and never fear.

There was a strong part of me that was quite excited about becoming a powerful spiritual being who would impress people. I envisioned myself standing on hilltops and preaching to hungry masses. I would walk on water and heal the sick. I was an egotistical monster who joined the spiritual path partly because the Prophets said it was the hardest road life had to offer, and I didn't like someone telling me it was too hard for me.

So what does an egotistical monster do when he starts the spiritual journey...he jumps in with both feet. That day, I gave up booze, drugs, sex, meat, sugar, and pretty much every "worldly distraction." Please note that although this worked for me, I am not suggesting this is necessary for anyone else. While sitting in that field in Montana I didn't have a clue what religion was asking of me. If I did, I probably would have run in fear, but I saw a sense of peace in that statue of Buddha, I heard an otherworldly message in the statements by Christ, I heard of endless possibilities in the writings of the various prophets, and I wanted to understand how they got there. They seemed to have found some understanding that the philosophers didn't, and my ego wanted the challenge and the knowledge to "better" itself.

I told myself I was going to search for the end of human suffering. It sounds counter-intuitive to join the spiritual path because your ego wanted to, but, in reality, I think that is how all people start. It seems counter-intuitive because "the path" is about defeating the ego not elevating it. But at first it doesn't matter where you get the impetuous; it only matters that you start. Getting rid of the ego comes later. In the meantime, I needed the ego in order to get the strength to repel old habits and distractions. There were thousands of times that I stayed in meditation with my back aching and my entire being screaming at me to go do something "fun," but I didn't because my ego was so determined not to fail or cower from this challenge.

Society misleads us by its use of the word "egotistical." We use that word to describe someone who has a rigorously self-confident personality. The reason why this is misleading is because it makes it appear that only these people are engulfed in an ego thereby leaving the rest of us somehow free from this egotistical beast. As I have stated earlier, the truth of the matter is that we are all engulfed in an ego. We are all egotistical. The only difference between the "egotistical," under the typical definition, and the rest of us is that the personalities we build are less irritating to other egos, or we have created a more sophisticated and harder to detect ego. We are all plagued with an ego all the same.

The word ego or id is the conglomerate of the various personalities we have created since childhood. Christ said, "Unless you change and become like little children, you will never enter the kingdom of heaven" (Matthew 18:3). He was saying you must become like you were when you were a child, prior to building an ego, in order to enter the bliss which is heaven. Buddha said the same thing when he said you must become selfless. Both were basically saying you must get rid of that confounded ego you have been creating all your life before you will find happiness.

The easiest way to state the big question is that the meaning of life is to become enlightened to the fact the ego is the cause of our suffering, and through that awareness you can work toward becoming completely liberated from the ego. Realizing what the meaning of life is isn't all that difficult. Becoming liberated is a bit more challenging. Actually, from the perspective of your ego, becoming liberated is a real pain in the ass. But, the rewards are definitely worth the trouble. Becoming enlightened is not difficult in the sense that it takes neither great physical strength nor great intellectual prowess. Anyone reading this book has the tools to become enlightened. All you need is the will, some basic knowledge, and the ability to pay attention. The road map is pretty straightforward and has been successfully navigated by many in the past.

You may be asking, "If the concept of enlightenment isn't so hard to grasp, then why isn't everyone already enlightened?" Well, that's a bit complicated. I believe it is because we have been sidetracked from birth by well-intentioned yet misinformed miscreants who we also call family and society. It isn't their fault. They, too, have been raised with the same misinformation. In addition, it is difficult to understand what the enlightened mind looks like from the perspective of the unenlightened. I'm not sure how God expected us to understand something that could only be understood once you get there, but I'll bring that up with him/her/it, whatever it is, when I get the opportunity. I have numerous complaints about his divine design (sunburn, sharks, evil, poop) just to name a few, which I'll address directly with the landlord himself.

One of our biggest problems with understanding enlightenment is that we lack the will to let go of the only existence we know, which is life experienced through this ego we created. Think about how difficult it is for you to give up the ego when you are currently living life through the ego. Why would it agree to these terms? The ego is, if we want to admit it or not, massively in control of our thoughts. If that is the case, how do we get it to agree it is the problem? You must commit mutiny and cast the captain from the ship. You must fire the boss. You must commit a hostile takeover of the company and a coup of the country.

Many people want to become enlightened, to an extent, but everyone is trying to bring their ego along for the ride. It can't work that way. The ego and enlightenment can't exist in the same space. There is a battle of good and evil going on in the world, and it is going on within you. The ego constantly wants something, and enlightenment is the state of not wanting or needing anything.

If you think you want enlightenment, then look at it this way. Think of someone you know in a bad marriage. You have probably thought that if that person just got out of that shitty relationship, they would probably be much happier. Well, I have news for you. Like it or not, we are all in a bad marriage. You and your ego don't make great companions. There are many instances when nobody wants to go to dinner with the two of you. We all have some married couples in our life that have caused us to say, "I like him/her, but their spouse annoys me." Well, I'm here to tell you that sometimes you are the one we like and sometimes you are the "other one." It all depends on how much of "you" or how much of your ego you are that day. We all like you, but your ego annoys the shit out of us.

119

So how do you divorce this bad spouse? How do you win the war of Armageddon? You must come to realize your ego is not the cause of your happiness but rather the block to your happiness. That friend of yours in the bad marriage is still in that marriage because they either think the good outweighs the bad, the pain of moving on is greater than the pain of staying, the fear of being alone is greater than the pain of staying, or they are simply too lazy to even think about it. These are the same reasons why people don't strive for enlightenment. We are all stuck in a bad marriage with our self.

Maybe I'm jumping the gun. There may be someone out there who believes they are in a healthy relationship with themselves. Let's pop that bubble first. Ask yourself if it feels good when people tell you that you are attractive, smart, creative, brave, strong etc. Does it feel good to be liked? Does it feel good to belong? Do you want to be thought of as a good person? Do you want to be remembered? Do you want to be successful? Has anyone ever made you mad? Has anyone every insulted you? Do you ever experience stress? Has any event made you sad? If you answered "yes" to any of these questions, then you are not in control of your happiness but rather your ego is in control. You are at the whim of others accepting you, liking you, judging you. Your happiness is conditional upon the whim of other people's ego.

Part of you knows what I am talking about, yet there is also a part of you that is arguing that it is only "natural" to experience these things. I will argue that it isn't natural or necessary. Your attachment to these experiences is due to your misguided belief that we should care what others think of us. Since birth you have been taught to care what others think. It benefits our ego's understanding of the world to care what others think. The ego needs others for companionship, for approval, for competition, etc. I need for you to need from me so I can hold that against you to get what I need from you. This is how the ego thinks.

The worst part is that we call this love. Trust me on this one. You will not be content nor will you be happy until you don't give a damn what others think of you. If you want a quick glimpse of the enlightened consciousness, then imagine for a second that you don't give a damn about ever being accepted by anyone every again. Did you feel it? Did you feel the liberation?

Did you feel the relief? If so, you are blessed with the ability to become enlightened right now and completely liberated in this life. You are that close. Now think, why would you ever go back to worrying? Why wouldn't you just stay in that bliss forever? "Who" within you has decided that you shouldn't? Think about that.

I am not preaching anti-social behavior. I am talking about liberation: truly free people who can be much better citizens because they are fearless and at peace. That is a society of enlightened people, which we can be. But, clearly, we are not.

I hate to put it this way, but we are all crack babies. Let's begin where we all got messed up. Imagine a baby fresh out of the womb. The doctor pulls out a needle and injects a little bit of crack into the baby. Every day, from that point forward, the parents inject the baby, or toddler, or child with crack. As the years go by the dosage increases with age and the ability to handle more crack. As a teenager the parents administer their crack and society injects excessive amounts more. Nobody questions this process because we have all been subjected to the same treatment. This is the way we have been raised.

Since birth the "crack" we have been fed is the lie that happiness is contingent upon the acceptance of others. That happiness is received through the love of a committed companion. That happiness is experienced by the accumulation of certain goods and by the respect of society, etc. We have been fed a false reality, but it has been injected in us since birth, and we now know no other. We are now addicted to a life and state of being which has an unquenchable thirst. We are addicts. We can never acquire enough. There is always someone else's approval to get. There is always someone's approval to keep. When we acquire something we must immediately begin our work at keeping it while simultaneously working towards the acquisition of the other things we desire or our loved one's desire. It never ends. Nor does the yearning of the crack head.

Please bear with me. I realize I have just called you a crack head in a dysfunctional marriage. Sorry about that, but do you believe the world is generally happy or unhappy, confused or enlightened, aware or searching, selfish or generous? If you believe that the world is generally unhappy and seeking awareness, then you must also realize that these same people raised you and taught you about how and why to live this life. We are confused adults raised by confused adults, and we are raising confused kids. This can be repaired. We can escape from the cycle of ignorance. We can become enlightened. It is easier than you think.

My brother once said an incredibly insightful thing to me. He said, "Imagine if you were drunk or high all the time, and you had never experienced sobriety during your entire life. Then someone came up with a pill that made you feel sober with a clear mind. You would pay a lot for that pill and want it all the time." Living with the ego is like being a junkie. You will always crave acceptance and be anxious of losing that acceptance. Enlightenment is being aware that reliance on the ego will always come with wanting, desiring, and the fear of loss. The enlightened realize how exhausting life with the ego is. The enlightened realize that a life liberated from constant cravings and anxiety is the goal.

Imagine not needing anything. Imagine not wishing for anyone's approval. Imagine not worrying that someone may fall out of love with you or worry they may decide to give their love to someone else. That is liberation. That is the state of existence you were meant for. That is the state of mind of the liberated. That is the goal of the enlightened. You can stay here with your fears or go to a state of fearlessness. It is up to you.

Less is More

"How would spirituality help a man of the world like me?" said the businessman. "It will help you have more." Said the master. "How?" "By teaching you to desire less."

Unknown Author

Selflessness

The devotee knelt to be initiated into discipleship. The guru whispered the sacred mantra into his ear, warning him not to reveal it to anyone. "What will happen if I do?" asked the devotee. Said the guru, "Anyone you reveal the mantra to will be liberated from the bondage of ignorance and suffering, but you yourself will be excluded from discipleship and suffer damnation." No sooner had he heard those words, then the devotee rushed to the marketplace, collected a large crowd around him, and repeated the sacred mantra for all to hear. The disciples later reported this to the guru and demanded that the man be expelled from the monastery for his disobedience. The guru smiled and said, "He has no need of anything I can teach. His action has shown him to be a guru in his own right."

Unknown Author

CHAPTER ELEVEN

1988 was the longest summer of my life. I could not wait for September. It meant an entire eight weeks of no partying and trying to hold onto the will to try this new course. I did it. I amazed myself. There were times I was so tempted to just say, "Oh, what the hell." It would be easier to have a cocktail and do a little bit of partying with the fellas than to put up with all the questions. But each time a little voice in my head would say, "Come on...you can do it...just hang in there." And I did; I just hung in there.

It wasn't that I was some kind of raving alcoholic, but, rather, it was the entire redirection of my life. It was having the trust that this new life would be satisfying, that this new life would have pleasure. This new path required me to give up all the sources of pleasure I currently knew and replace them with a far more refined understanding of pleasure, the pleasure of growing to be a better person.

All I knew at this point in life was to string together a day of jumping from one immediate gratification to the next. I would awake and drink coffee, eat breakfast, watch TV, get high, go for a bike ride, eat lunch, get attention, get drunk, have sex, watch a movie. Do it again tomorrow. None of these activities were available at the commune. I had to completely re-discover joy. That is what was scaring the shit out of me.

So, I showed up in Montana and there were approximately eighty students entering the twelve-week course. We were each given a roommate, and off we were carted to various rinky-dink doublewide trailers set off in some field. "Well," I thought, "what do you expect from a cult in Montana?"

The next day we were bused to a cafeteria where we were served miso soup (fermented soybeans), brown rice, boiled vegetables, and toast. "Wow, I thought, "This place is amazing. I've already lost my attachment to eating. This won't be hard at all. Simply make the food disgusting and the world unreachable, and soon I'll be craving meditation simply to keep amused."

After "breakfast" we headed to our "classroom." By "classroom," I mean a huge, blue, rectangular, sheet-metal barn surrounded by mobile homes or trailers as they are called in Montana. So now I am at a "cult" in a "trailer park." I thought, "All my dreams are coming true." As a kid from Jersey this was one of the last places I thought I would end up. I certainly began to doubt my choices.

From the outside the building looked like a large airplane hangar. It was about sixty yards long and thirty yards wide. Inside it was one large, cold, empty room. It had a cement floor, exposed heating, air conditioning ducts, and rows of blue cushioned, metal-framed chairs. On one end of the room there was a large stage or altar filled with religious icons from various religions. I think it was the first time I had ever seen a statue of Mother Mary only a few feet away from a statue of Buddha. It was strange. There were dozens of other figures on the altar, but I didn't recognize the rest of them because, in truth, I knew almost nothing about religions.

After I took a seat, in my childish, passive-aggressive way in the very last row, our instructor informed us that during the next twelve weeks we would be taught the teachings of the major religions combined with hours of practicing the prayers and techniques used by these religions. She stated that, "All of the major religious are saying the same thing. Everyone can and should become enlightened. We will discuss what this means and, more importantly, show you the various religious techniques that will assist you along the way like prayer, mantras, meditation, etc. So without further ado," she began, "please make yourself comfortable and prepare for a life changing, mind blowing twelve weeks." Even with the wise disclaimer of the instructor, there was no way I could have prepared myself for the emotional and physical pain that was coming my way. It was the most difficult twelve weeks of my life.

Every day I endured three tasteless meals noticeably void of any sugar, caffeine, meat, dairy products, or flavor. I'm not sure, but I think that only leaves dirt as a possible menu item. Actually, I can recall brown rice making up about 50% of every meal while the other 50% was made up of vegetables and beans of some sort. Yum, Yum, Yum. I won't even begin to explain what this does to the digestive tract of a kid raised on processed cereal, powdered potatoes, and pizza. Trust me, you don't want to know! And, to think, I paid thousands of dollars for this experience.

Our classes sometimes ran from 9:00am t

Yes, *midnight*...not noon...I said midnight. Each day   _gin with a different type of prayer. These were either Buddhist mantras in Cantonese or Hindu *bhajans* in Hindi or Christian prayers in English. Then we would hear a lecture and then back to another type of prayer and then to a tasteless meal and then a lecture and then a meditation and another tasteless meal then yoga and back and forth into the evening. The lectures consisted of every aspect of the spiritual path from every possible perspective. I heard about religions I never even knew existed. Have you ever heard of a religion called Zoroastrianism? I mean, come on, Zoroastrianism??? What is that? When the instructor first mentioned Zoroastrianism I leaned over to the guy next to me and cracked a joke saying, "Is that a religion started by a group of Mexicans that follow the legend of Zorro and instead of making the sign of the cross like Christians they move their hand back and forth really fast like they are making the sign of a Z with a sword?" He just gave me a quick, demeaning glance and then went back to his indignant "I'm holier than you look."

Day after day I showed up. I sat and I prayed in various languages, did hours of meditation, listened to lecture after lecture, and read the endless pages of religious stuff. It was an intellectual and emotional marathon. As each mystery of life was discussed, the question in my head which had been saying, "What is the meaning of life" began to change to, "Holy shit, how am I going to remember all this crap?" I began to believe that maybe I could obtain that peaceful liberated look on that Buddha statue, or maybe I could comprehend the peace and wisdom I heard in the sayings of the various prophets. Life began to change from a pointless ritualistic march towards death to a magical adventure.

Instead of a world of mindless sheep grazing on sports cars and Rolexes, I began to see a world filled with people just waiting to wake up from a long dream. Life was becoming a tremendous challenge, which seemed almost too daunting to accomplish. I became enthralled by the challenge of "growing spiritually." And my criticism of religion changed to deep admiration for anyone willing to try to wrestle with what it had to offer. Religion was no longer a path of hiding from your fears but rather a path of challenging and overcoming all of them.

Silence

Four Zen monks decided to meditate silently without speaking for two weeks. By nightfall on the first day, the candle began to flicker and then went out.

The first monk said, "Oh, no! The candle is out."

The second monk said, "Aren't we not supposed to talk?"

The third monk said, "Why must you two break the silence?"

The fourth monk laughed and said, "Ha! I'm the only one who didn't speak."

Unknown Author

CHAPTER TWELVE

Is there a God? Why are we here? Is there a heaven? Is reincarnation true? Are there angels? Continue to list all the existential question you may have. Let me tackle the God question by quoting one of the most famous Christian theologians, Thomas Aquinas. Then I'll let Buddha answer the remaining questions.

Thomas Aquinas wrote plenty during his life regarding the interpretation of the scripture and was one of the greatest influences on modern Christian theology. It was his last book, *Summa Theologica*, which was regarded as his greatest contribution to Christian thought. I will argue that his most important contribution was his assertion that "we cannot know what God is." It is my favorite definition of God. To know God is to know God as unknowable. Very few wiser things have ever been said.

Thomas was wisely telling us that God cannot be captured in human thought or words. If God exists, how God exists, where, etc., simply cannot be answered. He is instructing us to go forward in peace, knowing these questions cannot be answered, and live life. In addition, this statement naturally comes with the caveat that instructs us to stop wasting our time trying to define something unknowable. Does it make sense to spend time trying to do something that cannot be done? No. Move on, and spend your life on things that can improve your life like, might I suggest, understanding the destructive effects of your ego?

The remainder of your existential questions can all be answered by Buddha. Legend has it that one day Buddha was confronted by a typical existential procrastinator. This guy interrupted one of Buddha's lectures and asked, and I'll paraphrase, "Hey Buddha, why should I listen to you if you can't tell me why we are here and where will we go when we die?"

Buddha replied by telling the story now commonly referred to as the poison arrow story. Buddha said, "It's just as if a man were wounded with an arrow thickly smeared with poison. His friends and companions, kinsmen and relatives would provide him with a surgeon, and the man would say, 'I won't have this arrow removed until I know whether the man who wounded me was a noble warrior, a priest, a merchant, or a worker.' He would say, 'I won't have this arrow removed until I know the given name and clan name of the man who wounded me... until I know whether he was tall, medium, or short... until I know whether he was dark, ruddy-brown, or golden-colored... until I know his home village, town, or city... until I know whether the bow with which I was wounded was a long bow or a crossbow... until I know whether the bowstring with which I was wounded was fiber, bamboo threads, sinew, hemp, or bark... until I know whether the shaft with which I was wounded was wild or cultivated... until I know whether the feathers of the shaft with which I was wounded were those of a vulture, a stork, a hawk, a peacock, or another bird... until I know whether the shaft with which I was wounded was bound with the sinew of an ox, a water buffalo, a langur, or a monkey.' He would say, 'I won't have this arrow removed until I know whether the shaft with which I was wounded was that of a common arrow, a curved arrow, a barbed, a calf-toothed, or an oleander arrow.' The man would die and those things would still remain unknown to him." —Cula-Malunkyovada Sutta: The Shorter Instructions to Malunkya" (MN 63), Majjhima Nikaya.

Referring to this man Buddha then stated, "If he were to wait until all these questions have been answered, the man might die first." —Nhat Hanh, Thich; Philip Kapleau (2005). *Zen Keys*. Three Leaves Press. p. 42.

Essentially Buddha is telling us to stop wasting time on metaphysical questions that cannot be answered. Use your time here in life to answer what can be answered. To address your suffering, your fear, your anxiety, your rejection, your bizarre interpretation of love, the things that impinge your happiness, etc. These things can be answered. These illnesses can be healed. These arrows can be removed. Removing these ills is the next step. It is only logical for us to fix what we can. To not address what can be addressed because we cannot answer the unanswerable is a silly tactic of the ego to prolong your ignorance and its existence.

Remember, the ego doesn't want to be discovered. The ego doesn't want to be rejected by you. It doesn't want to give up control of your mind, your life, its life. It doesn't want to give up the driver's seat. It doesn't want you to realize it is the cause of all of your suffering. It doesn't want you to figure out that it has hijacked your mind, your body, your life, and that you have become its slave. If you figure out what it is doing to you, then surely you will reject it.

Without your reliance on it and devotion to it, the ego will die. Your attention to it is the nourishment that keeps it alive. Your belief that it is real, that the ego is you, and that you need its bullshit personalities to feel safe is how *your* devil stays alive. It will fight against your enlightenment as if it is fighting for its life...because it is fighting for its life. Remember that enlightenment is realizing your ego is the problem. Liberation is the final extinction of your ego. If you become enlightened, then the ego's time is limited. It must fight your enlightenment if it is to survive.

In order to distract you the ego uses some interesting tricks. When you are confronted with the path of enlightenment, it will first say, "This is bullshit. Let's go get a beer." Well, that's what mine said. If it cannot lead you away from the liberating message of enlightenment, then it tries to hijack your entire path by saying, "Yeah, this enlightenment stuff is awesome. Let's do this." Then it will proceed to make enlightenment about glorifying itself. It will appear wholeheartedly interested in enlightenment. It will pacify you by pretending you are engaging in enlightenment. It may say the prayers and attend the rituals, but it is not really engaged or trying to become enlightened. It is simply doing this to pacify you, to make you think you are doing something good. This way it can survive another day. I call it spiritual judo. In Judo the student is taught to use the momentum of the attacker against them. If you charge they use your forward motion to throw you in that direction. The ego uses Judo all the time. If you want to go a certain direction, and it realizes it can't fight you, it will agree and then hijack the experience to make sure you don't realize the ego is the problem. Look how many religious people are pompous asses? I'm sorry, but it happens way more often than a person who finds religion and immediately become a humble follower. Most people immediately become proud of their newfound religious conviction. They typically feel superior to those not on "the path." This is because the ego told them that they were doing the "right" thing.

Like I said earlier, maybe this is the only way for humans to start the path toward enlightenment. The problem is when the student never realizes their ego is taking them for a ride. They jump into religion with both feet and feel elated. Then over time the passion fizzles due to a lack of personal "progress," and they lose interest. Perfect, the ego won. The entire journey was directed by the ego and the student never realized they were duped. They never realized they were meant to turn the powerful tools of mediation and prayer, which should heighten awareness, where directed, like a spot light, upon the devil himself, which is inside us, which is our ego. If the spot light is controlled by the ego, then the devil stands out of sight where it is safe and communicates to the soul that the coast is clear.

This is the most common path for those who stick around and explore enlightenment. They follow the ego into a useless holding pattern using spiritual concepts and phrases while internally saying, "Look how spiritual I am. What a great person I am. I'm surely going to heaven. I'm better than others. I'm so wise. Blah blah blah." Nothing accomplished. You simply gave your ego a new expression to glorify itself: spiritual pride, the main killer of the student on the path toward enlightenment.

With this the ego has accomplished two main objectives. First, it keeps you from becoming enlightened, and it remains the captain of your consciousness. The typical religious person misses this point because they are looking outward when the entire battle is inward. Christ clearly told his students that the devil was within. In his Sermon on the Mount he stated, "If thy right eye offend pluck it out (the enemy, the problem, where you should look to become liberated is within you). It is profitable that one of thy members perish (the ego) and not the whole body be cast into hell" (Matthew 5:30) (don't associate/identify with the ego lest it drag you into attachment/suffering/hell). These followers somehow came up with an interpretation and propagated the theory that there is an external being called the devil that we all must be on guard against, and if we continue to pray to Jesus, the devil can't get us and we will be safe. This is what happens when the ego is in charge of what we hear. It will take a very simple message about it being the problem and redirect the attention somewhere other than itself. Christ clearly stated that the obstacle to entering bliss (the kingdom of heaven) is in our mind and the way we are thinking, and the ego heard it and redirected the message by claiming it was not the culprit nor internal at all but rather "over there." The ego sent us on a wild goose chase whereby we have been running away from this imaginary exterior devil for 2,000 years while it sat happily and safely within us.

141

As Christ stated in Luke 12:51, "Suppose ye that I came to give peace in the earth? I tell you, nay; but only division. (Division is you from your ego) For from this time forth, five in one house (your ego's personality traits) will be divided, three against two, and two against three, they will be divided, father against son, and son against father, mother against daughter, and daughter against the mother; mother-in-law against daughter-in-law, and daughter-in-law against the mother-in-law."

And in Luke 12:54 Christ states, "You learned to judge the weather, you've studied the world but not yourself (Yourself: meaning, your own ego). Hypocrites, for when thou are with thine adversary (ego) give diligence (carefully analyze what it is offering) that thou mayest be delivered from him lest he drag thee to the judge (get rid of the ego and see its flaws, or he will drag you back to relying on social acceptance/attachment/judgment) and the judge deliver thee to the exactor and the exactor cast thee into prison (you become its victim and fall back into believing that you need the ego and its attachments). I say to thee, thou shalt not depart thence (be removed from your prison or bad marriage to the ego) till thou hast paid the very last mite (overcome every last, even smallest of attachments)."

In Matthew 10:34 Christ states, "I did not come to send peace to earth...but with a sword. I came to set man at variance with his father and a man's foes will be they of his household." When Christ describes "household," he is talking about you. That is how he describes "you" which entails your soul, your ego, all its personalities, etc. "Man's foes will be they of his household." Christ is telling us that our "foe" is within us. Christ came with a sword (message to cut us free from the ego) to set man at variance... (to make us aware of our opposing interest with the ego).

Your soul and the ego each have a path that they are trying to sell you. You are always at a fork in the road. Your soul's path starts by becoming enlightened to the fact that your ego's way of seeking happiness is flawed because it is tainted with attachment, which leads to perpetual fear of losing that which you believe you "need" for happiness. I define the enlightened as a person who becomes aware of the truth: the soul is perfect and the obstacle to experiencing that perfection is the ego.

Once you become enlightened to this fact you begin to unravel your ego's grip on your life. By observing the unhappiness that results from the ego's way of living, you will realize it has only unhappiness to offer. You slowly begin to drop your attachments and begin to experience a life where you "need" less, fear less, feel rejected less, are offended less often, and enter the road toward complete liberation from these unnecessary obstacles to happiness.

There will even be a time when you no longer fear death. Matthew 10:38 says, "He that finds life shall lose it (you only experience loss if you are attached) and he that loses his life (loses his attachment to life and fear of death) for my name sake shall find it." What does Christ mean by "find" life? He means to truly live life. To enjoy it as only someone who has no fear of death can enjoy life. Imagine how any experience is depleted if you are experiencing the fear of it ending, or the fear of losing it. This is true of all experiences in life. Your marriage or relationships are damaged by the fear of being rejected. Your enjoyment of your children is damaged by your fear of their injury, death, or rejection. The enjoyment of every moment is decreased by your fear of your finances, losing your job, losing your health, and losing your life.

Many people argue that it is "natural" to fear these things. They argue that you aren't human if you lose your attachments and the fears that naturally come with attachments. Well, they are dead wrong. Imagine how enjoyable a life without fear would be. You would be busting with joy and taking life by the horns. I can prove it isn't necessary to live in fear because people, even those who are not liberated, live in various degrees of fear every day.

Does everyone on the planet have the same exact fear of financial instability, social rejection, or death? No. This means that it is not the event that causes the reaction but rather you that decides its affect. It is not dictated by life but rather your subjective decision. The fact that people have the freedom to react differently proves that you are in control of the degree of the reaction all the way to the point of fearlessness. You can choose, and people do it every day, not to fear these things at all.

I love the story of the man who was being chased by a tiger. He was running for his life, and the tiger was hot on his heels. He was so consumed with the tiger he failed to notice an approaching cliff, and he accidentally runs off its edge. While falling, he reaches out and grabs hold of a branch from a bush

THE MEANING OF LIFE: ONE MAN'S JOURNEY AND DISCOVERY OF LIFE'S MOST IMPORTANT QUESTION

growing on the side of the mountain, which stops his fall. He looks down and sees the valley floor 1,000 feet below him. He looks up and sees the tiger waiting for him. If he climbs up, he gets eaten, and when his arm tires, he falls to his death. Either way he goes to certain death. Now realizing that his life will soon be over he looks at the bush and finds a berry growing on it. As the story goes, he plucks the berry and puts it in his mouth, pauses and thinks, "Never has anything ever tasted so good."

Why? Because he had nothing to lose. It was all lost already. At that moment he was free of all financial woes, social obligations, expectations, worry, regret, attachments, etc. He was liberated. He was, for the first time, in the moment and truly "free." All his faculties were present and he tasted liberation and how beautiful each moment of existence is once you drop all your attachments and fears. This is what Christ meant by "finding life." What he is telling us is that we are all capable of a blissful life free of fear all the time. We are all capable of "entering the kingdom of heaven" which is a state of fearlessness and bliss. Why are we all choosing the path of fear which Christ calls "hell?"

Why? The ego, it would seem, is a much better salesman. It has a shittier product but somehow is selling the "hell" out of it. Billions of people are marching blindly down its road of fear and attachment. How is this possible? Well, remember when I called you a crack baby? Yep, it's the crack that is blinding us. It is the process that the ego goes through that we have been fed and have become addicted to. It is the yearning and the hope that we may get what we want and then the fear of losing it. This rollercoaster of emotions is the high we are addicted to. In addition, nobody is discussing the alternative. Nobody believes that fearlessness is even an option. How many people in your life have said, "Ya know, you have the option of not fearing anything." No one. Even the religious people, who were supposed to be teaching you this path of fearlessness, are adding fears to your life. They are telling you that you "Better be a good Christian. You better be careful or the devil will get you. Be good or you will end up in hell for eternity." Where they came up with this shit is beyond me. But, it is complete bullshit!

Beyond Rules

Two traveling Zen monks reached a river where they met a young woman. Wary of the current, she asked if they could carry her across. One of the monks hesitated, but the other quickly picked her up onto his shoulders, transported her across the water, and put her down on the other bank.

She thanked him and departed.

As the monks continued on their way, the one was brooding and preoccupied. Unable to hold his silence, he spoke out.

"Brother, our spiritual training teaches us to avoid any contact with women, but you picked that one up on your shoulders and carried her!"

"Brother," the second monk replied, "I set her down on the other side, while you are still carrying her."

Unknown Author

CHAPTER THIRTEEN

The three-month course in Montana was ending in a week. It was the first week of December 1988 and once again I began to fear getting kicked out of the cult. I must be the only person who has worried about this. When the class was finished, I would have to go back out into the world. How, I wondered, am I going to keep up my march towards enlightenment on the streets of this world? I have been celibate and sober for six months, and it no longer was making my skin crawl. I really felt like I could continue the monastic life without wanting to hit my head against the wall. I learned to truly enjoy meditating and even praying. I learned to sit and pray for up to eight hours with only one or two breaks to go to the bathroom or to grab a quick cup of tea.

I began to feel a power from these rituals I never felt before. It makes you high and gives you a feeling of otherworldly power. I would have amazingly vivid dreams of beautiful places filled with a tremendous presence of peace. It seemed to me that it

149

would be much easier to keep this lifestyle here at this secluded place in Montana than it would be on the campus at the University of Colorado or anywhere else I could think of. I knew that if I went back out into the world, I would be able to sustain this for a while but not forever. I simply didn't have the discipline. My desires were too strong to resist the distractions put right in front of me. I needed more time.

So I wrote to the cult leaders, begging them to let me stay. A week later I got a letter telling me they didn't want me, and I had to leave when the class was over. I was stunned. I must be the only person on the planet that has been rejected by a cult twice! For the love of God, what does a guy have to do? I always thought these cult people were running around abducting people. I'm begging to get abducted, and they keep telling me to bug off. I guess I needed to find a more desperate cult.

So off I went. I drove to my mother's house in the foothills of Boulder, Colorado and hunkered down. I woke every morning and did hours of prayers in order to armor myself for the day. After several weeks I became bored, and my prayers became more arduous. I hopped in my car and drove to New Jersey to hang out with my old friends. I got a job waiting tables and got a room with my old buddy from high school. Exactly what I feared began to happen. The weight of the world, my old habits, and my temptations began to take hold. My prayers, which I tried to do in my car or my bedroom out of the public eye, were not giving me the high and elation I experienced back in Montana. I just didn't have the support of hundreds of people living the same lifestyle.

In Montana I didn't have to worry about the normal burdens of a twenty-one-year-old. They supplied everything; room, board, healthcare, education, a serious dearth of hot chicks (there may have been two girls my age out of the 700 commune inhabitants), no booze, no typical worldly distractions. You also had 33,000 acres of pristine Rocky Mountains to wander at your leisure.

After about four months I wrote the commune again and said, "I'm not making it out here. I know if I stay here I'll be back to the normal distractions of your average twenty-one-year-old by year's end. This whole spiritual thing will be a little fanatical blip on the screen of this life. I'll never be sure I'll ever get back to it."

THE MEANING OF LIFE: ONE MAN'S JOURNEY AND DISCOVERY OF LIFE'S MOST IMPORTANT QUESTION

I knew that the possibility of where it could have taken me would haunt me the rest of my life.

Well, third time was a charm. The cult called and asked me if I wanted to help build bomb shelters because they feared the U.S. might be bombed by nuclear weapons someday. At that point I would have helped them build a freaking ark if they asked. I just wanted to get my ass out of Jersey and back in the protected confines of the commune.

This is when I began to realize the bad stuff going on at the commune that did make it pretty cult like. The leader began introducing crazy beliefs about the end of the world, the evils of rock music, sex, alcohol, and the world in general. She encouraged people to not communicate with their family outside the church and tried to move her role from teacher to infallible guru. Several years later she was diagnosed with Alzheimer's, and many think that she became increasingly radical due to the onset of her illness. Who knows?

I was fortunate that I was just a kid who they used to do construction, work on the farm, and fix roads or whatever else they needed. I really didn't get involved with policymaking, theological direction, or other weird stuff. I woke, went to prayer, ate breakfast, went to work, went to prayer, and went to bed every day alongside of some of the sweetest and most thoughtful people I have ever met, many whom I keep in contact with and consider my closest friends.

I lived at the commune for approximately two years. It was pretty much the same routine every day: sleep, pray, eat, work, eat, pray, lecture, sleep. No booze, no TV, no sex, no worldly anything. Two extremely important events happened to me during those years. One was a slow gentle adjustment, and the other was a radical jolt. The gentle adjustment was the most profound and longest lasting. I slowly lost my addiction to constant distraction. I used to wake up, and my first thought was how I was going to orchestrate a day of one pleasure or distraction after another: what would I have for breakfast, then I'll smoke some weed, go to work if I must, bartending wasn't so tough if you drink while you do it, hang out with friends, have a few more drinks, go to bed, and start all over again.

After almost three years now of learning to sit still without a TV, radio, or anything to entertain me was like emotional bodybuilding. I was slowly learning to concentrate, to focus, to listen to my thoughts and the world around me. I quieted the constant clamoring in my head for pleasure from the world around me. The ascetic life starves those desires until they die on the vine. I learned tools of prayer, mediation, and most importantly, observation without allowing my ego to completely control my internal monologue.

I am not saying that all people need to move off to a commune or monastery in order to conquer the senses, but I know I needed it. I think I was just a more difficult case than most. I might have been able to do it in the world but not at the pace that complete abstention provided.

The radical event that I gained from the commune happened the day after my twenty fourth birthday on September 15, 1990. For my birthday I decided to go up into the mountains for five days of fasting and mediation. I had recently read of an eastern saint who claimed he was able to leave his body during sleep and travel throughout the world and to different plains of physical and emotion states. I thought that would be fun, so I thought I would try it.

I grabbed a backpack and five miso-almond-grain "cookies," a loaf of bread, and a jar of almond butter and headed several miles into the mountains just north of Yellowstone Park by a little lake. I set up camp, and it was my intention to only eat one cookie per day and to pray and mediate as many hours as I could stand.

The first night was not very spiritual. I hiked about halfway to my intended campsite and the sun began to set. I decided it was not worth setting up an entire camp, so I just slept on the ground in my sleeping bag next to my back pack. Sleeping in grizzly country out in the open can be a bit unnerving, especially in the fall when the bears become a bit more aggressive about fattening up for winter.

Well, apparently in the night it got so cold that I cinched my sleeping bag completely closed around my head in an attempt to stay warm. In the early morning hours I awoke due to a nightmare that I was about to be eaten by a grizzly bear who was holding me in his two paws like the burrito I resembled due to my cocooned-sleeping bag-enwrapped state. I really wish there was a camera to capture my frantic attempt to free myself from my

155

entombment and the imaginary jaws of the giant grizzly. It took me a good minute to find the hole at the end of the bag as I twisted and tried to escape. It all ended with me breathing heavily, sweaty, sitting on a lovely mountain top having a good laugh after the pure panic washed away.

On the next evening after I set up camp I prayed for several hours and went to my tent. I lay there trying to get out of my body. I wasn't sure exactly how to do this, so I visualized my "soul" wiggling as if it was trying to get out of a sleeping bag in a far more peaceful way than I did the morning before. It now seems kind of dumb, but the guy who claimed to do it didn't give any instructions how to get started. Well, the next thing I knew it was morning, and I'm pretty sure I just dreamed about food all night. I'm almost positive I didn't fly around the world nor visit other plains of existence. If I did, I have no recollection of it.

For the next three days I followed the same routine. I would arise, pray for several hours, go eat that one delicious cookie (very slowly), go for a hike, read, pray for several more hours, hop in my tent, wiggle around, trying to get out of my body, fail miserably, wake up starving after dreaming about food all night. On the fourth morning something felt different. Every day, up to this point, I would immediately get a great high from praying. But that day it didn't happen. I was stuck in a funk. For the last three days I was just giddy and felt high as a kite. I had a smile pasted on my face and felt like I could almost fly. I was sitting on mountaintops looking out over thousands of acres of wilderness with my feet dangling over cliffs with 100s or 1,000-foot drops. The weather was perfect, and I felt on top of the world.

But that day I felt depressed. I sat by the same tree and did the same prayers I did every other morning. But that day they weren't working. After an hour or two I began to think "Maybe I have been fasting too long. Maybe my blood sugar is too wacked for me to feel okay." I brought the loaf of bread and the almond butter just in case the fasting thing wasn't working and I needed the energy to hike back to civilization. Since I was in grizzly country I hung the food a half-mile from my tent in a tree. As I walked towards the food a part of me got excited about eating while another part of me was upset that I was giving up on my commitment to fast the entire five days.

Throughout my entire life I never really experienced depression. I always had tremendous sympathy for those that do. But I felt for the first time that maybe this is how they feel. As I walked along I felt so "blah." It was a feeling I really have never felt before, and it was strong. Part of me was still arguing that if I would just eat a little, that should cure it, and then I can get back to my mission of wiggling out of my body. But the other argument in my head began to gather steam. It began to say, "Wait a minute, just because this fasting thing is getting hard doesn't mean that you should give up on it...chicken...pansy...pussy." That got me pissed off. Enough so that I began to think, "Maybe I shouldn't eat no matter how miserable I am. Maybe I should stick it out?" That set off a proverbial war of emotions. Part of me had already committed to the pleasure I was going to get from eating and, trust me, I was really, really hungry. I had been eating those little stupid cookies for four freaking days, and I needed to eat something...NOW!

The other voice was still pushing the "pansy/wimp" argument, which progressed to, "Look what you have done your entire life when you didn't like the way you felt...you medicated. I don't care if it was with booze, drugs, sex, TV, or a God damn real cookie, but that is what you have done, and that is what you are trying to do here. You are just trying to medicate and make this uncomfortable feeling go away. How are you going to understand this feeling and understand why you feel this way if you medicate it away?" Damn it! Now it used a logic I came to embrace. I was doing all this to better understand my feelings, especially when it came to my attachments and desires. How can I run from this feeling even though it is one of the most annoying and depressing moments of my life?

Well, I stopped walking towards the food. I was beginning to agree with the voice telling me to confront this depression. This may sound silly, but turning back toward my camping spot without the food was one of the hardest things I ever had to do in my life. There was so much emotion committed towards pacifying that angst. Turning into it was like swimming up the Yellowstone River.

About halfway back to my tent something extremely strange happened. I can't explain how it happened, but I understand why it happened, and that is all that matters. I was walking along, and all the sudden a vision of a house appeared before me. I was shocked. I was awake and walking through the woods, but at the same time there was a house in front of me. When this happened I decided I better sit down on a nearby fallen tree so I wouldn't trip and fall on my face. Once I got situated and stopped worrying if I was having a stroke, I realized I didn't feel depressed anymore. It had moved "outside" of me. I could sense the depression, and it was coming from the house in my vision. I thought, "Great, I've exchanged depression for insanity."

So there I was in the woods, on the edge of a field, about 100 yards from my campsite, sitting on a fallen tree with a vision of a house before me. The house appeared about 50 feet away, and I was looking right at the front door from the street. As I said, I no longer felt depressed, but I detected the depression I was feeling, and it was coming from the house.

I decided to walk up to the house and investigate the source of the depression. It was a typical white farmhouse with blue shutters and a large front yard with a tree and a bush. It had a stone walkway, which was slightly overgrown with grass and a grey-shingled roof. I walked up to the plain white door and pushed it open. I looked down a hallway with a wooden floor and white walls that lead back to what looked like a kitchen. The entire house was dimly lit and appeared uninhabited and not well maintained. To the right was a sitting room. To the immediate left was a staircase leading upstairs over the kitchen and a living room.

I felt that the depression was coming from down the hall, so I stepped into the house and walked halfway down the hallway towards the kitchen. There I saw a door on my right. I felt the depression was coming from behind the door. I opened the door with trepidation, not fully knowing what I was going to see. The door opened to a large wooden staircase leading down to what appeared to be a poorly lit basement with a cement floor and no apparent furnishing or windows. I walked to the bottom of the stairs and waited for my eyes to adjust to the dark room.

As my eyes adjusted I saw what appeared to be a cage about four feet tall and four feet wide. Then I saw something in the cage, and as I stepped closer I realized it was a little boy. He was about four years old, dirty, cold, under nourished, very frightened and dressed in nothing but a pair of old, dirty, white underwear that were so tattered they were barely hanging on. He cowered in the far back corner as I approached. I spoke softly in order to comfort him. I kept saying, "It's alright, I won't hurt you. I slowly reached the cage and undid the latch and slowly lifted the caged lid. I reached in and stroked his head, and when I saw he became more at ease, I reached under his arms and lifted him up. When he wrapped his arms around my neck, it was so tight I thought he would choke me. When I felt him against my chest I felt like my heart was going to explode. Both of us began to cry.

My tears quickly turned to anger as I began to wonder why this little boy was down here? Who was neglecting this little boy? Who could be so mean? As I was contemplating these questions I began to feel a presence behind me, and I quickly turned back towards the staircase. Through the staircase I saw a person. He was about seven feet tall, he had pale skin that looked like it had never seen the sun. He was wearing leather boots, torn, dirty jeans with a big belt buckle with some stupid insignia I didn't bother to make out. He was wearing a black leather vest that was unbuttoned, and his huge pale belly hung way over his pants. He was a big, hairy, nasty human being.

I was so infuriated I didn't care how big or scary he was. I wanted to tear him limb from limb for torturing this little sweet child. When I looked him in the eye, in my rage I saw that he was actually afraid and was standing behind the stairs to protect himself from being discovered by me. I just stood there holding that little boy while standing in the basement of this strange imaginary house looking at a monster cowering from me. I looked upward and I said "God, what the hell is going on. What is this?"

The stairs and the house began to become transparent, and I was looking at a huge spine that reached up towards the sky and disappeared in the dark sky. For some reason I suddenly realized I was standing inside myself. I was in the belly, or the basement, of myself. I was holding my soul, and the monster behind the staircase was my ego. This was a graphic depiction of who I am. I realized I was the abuser. I created that ego that lives on gluttony, feeds off desires, and is inflated with self-importance. I am both a disgusting beast and a sweet innocent child. At this point in my life the beast was definitely in charge. Somehow I was granted this vision to better show me who I really was. How huge my reliance on the ego was. How conflicted are interest of the soul and the ego. How disgusting the needs, wants, and actions of the ego really are.

It was incredibly humbling to see what I was made of and how much of it was disgusting. I was 90% controlled by my ego even after all these years of prayer, mediation, and abstaining. I think I was granted the vision because I worked for it by turning from the distraction I craved when I almost broke my fast. That was the test. The reward for turning into the pain and resisting the ego's attempt to relieve its discomfort was the vision, which revealed to me my task for this life: become a good parent to that child; kill that ego; move my allegiance from egocentric living to the soul's selfless non-attachment.

As I realized what this vision was meant to tell me, it began to fade. As it faded I quickly tightened my embrace around the child, hoping he would stay, but his vision went with the house and the beast. Although the vision disappeared I swear I felt that child's arms around my neck for several days. At that point, I realized what I was meant to do with this life: slay that beast and free that child. To do this I would need to learn how to live without the need for that ego.

My time at the commune was done. It gave me the tools (prayer and meditation), the will power, the discipline, and the purpose I needed to continue the spiritual path no matter where I was or what I was doing. A few months later I hopped on a Greyhound bus with $100, a garbage bag of clothes, moved to Chicago, and enrolled in the Religious Studies program at DePaul University.

What we want or what we need?

There was once a hard-working and generous farmer who had several idle and greedy sons. On his deathbed he told them that they would find his treasure if they were to dig in a certain field. As soon as the old man was dead, the sons hurried to the fields, which they dug up from one end to another, and with increasing desperation and concentration when they did not find the gold in the place indicated.

But they found no gold at all. Realizing that in his generosity their father must have given his gold away during his lifetime, they abandoned their search. Finally, it occurred to them that, since the land had been prepared they might as well now sow a crop. They planted wheat, which produced an abundant yield. They sold this crop and prospered that year.

After the harvest was in, the sons thought again about the bare possibility that they might have missed the buried gold, so they again dug up the fields, with the same result. After several years they became accustomed to labor, and to the cycle of the seasons, something which they had not understood before. Now they understood the reason for their father's method of training them, and they became honest and contented farmers. Ultimately, they found themselves possessed of sufficient wealth and no longer to wonder about the hidden hoard.

Author Unknown

CHAPTER FOURTEEN

It is my experience that almost everyone, unbeknownst to themselves, worships the devil. It will be easy for me to win this argument since I get to define what the devil is. Before we define what the devil is, let us gain some awareness of how we view life. Most people find happiness in a day of no troubles, those peaceful days when nothing goes wrong, that day when there were no arguments and no headaches. Many people believe that these days are the good days, the days when "God smiled kindly on them." Well, this day may be a reward from God for the hard work you have done in the past, or it may be the "Devil's" handy work.

For now, think of the terms "God" and the "Devil" as metaphors. God will represent a force pushing you towards enlightenment, and the Devil will represent a force resisting enlightenment. I do not care if good and evil actually exist, but I am more interested in making the point that most people are not interested in enlightenment but rather interested in the "easy life" of not changing.

Many people believe that the good days are the days when our present understanding of ourselves was not challenged. The pleasant days when no one rocked our boat and everything went as planned. This is a day we all enjoy. We work very hard at having as many days like this as possible. But do these days help us grow, or do they assist us in staying the same? I realize that a life full of trials and tribulations may not be that helpful either because it would drive us so crazy that we would probably jump off a cliff. But I also know that people don't go out of their way to discover or question the way they look at the world unless that way of viewing the world is challenged. We just aren't that motivated as a species.

We all have a choice of how we want to become liberated. Ask yourself, "Do you want to grow through pain or pleasure?" Would you be surprised to learn that almost everyone chooses pain? Listen to my explanation and then admit to yourself if you are one of those people.

The average person doesn't walk through life looking for their flaws. They don't observe themselves constantly and say things like, "Did I just say that in order to hurt that person because they hurt me first? Am I acting this way because I'm afraid of losing him/her and that fear is causing me to try to control them? Am I doing this because I want people to be impressed by me or to get their approval? Are my religious views logical, or did I adopt them in order to pacify my fear of death or the unknown? Am I blaming him/her right now because I don't want to admit that I was wrong? Am I in this job because I love it or because I settled due to my financial insecurity? Am I staying in this unhappy marriage/relationship because I'm afraid of the unknown alternative?"

As you can imagine, the list of things that we could possibly be more honest about could be quite long. The confusing part for most people to grasp is that being honest about these things is the path of pleasure and not pain. Most people view such honesty as the path of pain because confronting our weaknesses and/or our insecurities is difficult and painful for most. If you believe that, then let me ask you this. What is more painful, spending an entire life in the wrong career or marriage or

169

confronting the reason for your decision and thereby admitting you are unhappy and moving on to a life that is more pleasing? Hopefully you answered the latter of the two. If you answered living in ignorance and perpetual dissatisfaction, then I can't help you.

These admissions are only painful because we are identifying with our ego. These admissions are pure pleasure to the soul. The unenlightened are convinced that the ego's wants and fears are their wants and fears. The unenlightened are "ego-centric," meaning they live from the perspective of the ego. They believe the ego is "self" in the first person. The enlightened hear the wants and fears of the ego, but they don't associate with them. They see how self-destructive they are. They simultaneously feel how liberating it is to the soul every time the ego's destructiveness is identified, and thereby the overall ego is diminished. The enlightened look for the ego's childish reactions, fearful inhibitions, and cruel self-serving actions in order to liberate the "self" from these destructive influences.

Although this seems to be obvious, it is the road less traveled. We accept long-term dissatisfaction to avoid the pain of admitting we were wrong. Why? The ego hates to admit it is wrong. The ego isn't even wired to admit fault. It is wired to blame others, to suffer delusions of grandeur, to deny any unflattering reality, to look right in the mirror, suck in its gut and say, "I'm not overweight," right after getting off the scale, which empirically stated the exact opposite. Do you really fight your ego at every turn or are you the typical person who would rather let it lie right now to avoid the work that admitting the truth would require?

Ninety-nine percent of the world lets the ego deny reality, feign ignorance, and/or lie outright on a daily basis without us even acknowledging it. The result is that we end up not being who we think we are: not being in the job we love, languishing in a marriage we don't enjoy, or compromising our values, our needs, our hopes, and dreams. We deny. We wait until we can't lie anymore and life catches up with us. Our spouse can't take the avoidance, the disinterest, the subtle sarcasm, the lack of passion, etc. Our boss complains about our lack of production, our mediocre effort, our disinterest. Soon our marriage is "on the rocks" and our job is in jeopardy and our liver hurts from drinking away reality. Is it really easier to live the life of avoidance and ignorance? Is it really more painful to be honest about who we are on a daily basis and confront that reality before we buy a house and have innocent children in a life we never wanted?

Are you growing through proactive analysis of your life or a reactionary let's-clean-up-this-mess type of approach? Most of us are unwittingly pulled along through life by our ego only to wake up one day in a life we are not satisfied with. We are all living with a long grocery list of delusion. We have been raised to believe that this was the only way to live. We were taught that if we just build the proper ego, it would get us the things we want in order to be happy. We built our own jail and jailer and never realized it. For that we are innocent. How we decide to break out of this jail is up to us. We can either do it quickly via an honest assessment of the existence of our ego and its flaws and thereby move on to happiness sooner, or we can stick our head back in the sand and wait for the unhappiness around us boil over into an undeniable reality and make the least amount of adjustment possible in order to stop the water from boiling over.

I love the story of the person who calls a therapist for help. When the therapist arrives they find the person standing in shit so deep they must stand on their tippy toes and tilt their head back in order to keep their nostrils out of the excrement and breathe. The therapist says to herself, "Oh my, let me reach in and pull this poor person out of this disgusting place." But the patient states, "Oh no, I don't want you to pull me out, but rather, I just want you to teach me how to keep the excrement from forming waves."

This is a horrifying depiction of the typical person, but it's true. We want to do the least amount necessary to maintain our status quo. We only make substantial changes because life was about to fall apart (divorce, lose our job, death, etc.). We don't want to see the truth. We don't want to admit who we are. We don't want to see the failings of our ego. We are choosing to make the least amount of admission and adjustment in order to make life tolerable, which, in the aggregate, is more painful than the work of proactively observing our words and actions and honestly admitting our childish ideas and attachments and thereby initiating positive change.

Father Anthony DeMello, one of my primary teachers on my journey toward enlightenment, liked to tell people they must begin the path towards enlightenment by realizing that they are a mess. He would ask his students, "Do you ever experience anxiety? If so, you are a mess. Do you ever get angry? If so, you are a mess. Do you ever fear? If so, you are a mess." What he was saying was, "Why are you still experiencing hurtful emotions when you don't have to?" You are all capable of liberating yourself from EVERY hurtful emotion, yet we are all still hanging onto the belief that if we just got better at acquiring things and holding onto them, it would solve all our problems. He tells us that we have the option of letting go of all desires and fears, but we choose not to. We choose the more painful path.

This is why I believe we are all worshiping the devil. We are praying for that new job, that big house, that gorgeous, kind spouse, those loving kids and that winning lottery ticket. Even the act of hoping for these things and believing they will make us happy is the cause of our suffering and constant anxiety. The devil I am referring to, our ego, wants to keep us in a present state of wanting. He wants us to continue believing happiness comes from desiring these things. He has a stick tied to our back and we are chasing the carrot he placed at the end of the string and it is constantly dangling just out of our reach. We fight hard every day to capture that carrot. We pray with earnest for assistance in getting that carrot. Who are we praying to? Do you think God wants to assist us in this destructive pattern? Do you think God wants to see us enslaved under the rule of this imaginary overlord that can only deliver suffering and unhappiness? Do you think God wants us to become free from all fear, anxiety, and pain like the enlightened, or does he want us to deepen our belief in the anxiety-filled process of believing that things, people, and acceptance are necessary for happiness?

God wants us to lose our attachments. God wants us to become liberated from that stick and carrot and lose our fears and pain. God wants this so bad that God doesn't care if we lose our house, our spouse, our job, our security. God wants one thing of us: enlightenment. If we want God on our side, then we should pray for one thing and one thing only: enlightenment. God really could care less about our comfort if that comfort will keep us ignorant and attached to the destructive reliance on our ego. Jesus did not come here to "send peace to the world but with a sword."

Wisdom

It always pleased the master to hear people recognize their ignorance. "Wisdom tends to grow in proportion to one's awareness of one's ignorance," he claimed. When asked for an explanation, he said, "When you come to see you are not as wise today as you thought you were yesterday, you are wiser today."

Teachings of Father Anthony DeMello

Do you really want what it takes?

The guru sat in meditation on the riverbank when a disciple bent down to place two enormous pearls at his feet, a token of reverence and devotion.

The guru opened his eyes, lifted one of the pearls, and held it so carelessly that it slipped out of his hand and rolled down the bank into the river.

The horrified disciple plunged in after it, but though he dived in again and again till late evening, he had no luck.

Finally, all wet and exhausted, he roused the guru from his meditation: "You saw where it fell. Show me the spot so I can get it back for you."

The guru lifted the other pearl, threw it into the river, and said, "Right there!"

Unknown Author

CHAPTER FIFTEEN

Over the next three years I finished my degree in Religious Studies. It gave me a good understand of religious text, conventional interpretations, and historical background, which was nice. It's helpful if your goal is academia, but if your goal is enlightenment, there's not much value. You can go to a church and get emotional dogma, or you can go to a university and get intellectual dogma. I realize it is strange to use those two words together, but the degree consisted of a lot of data memorization and regurgitation of other academics' misinterpretation of the scriptures. Still, anytime you get to debate any interpretation it has some merit.

While getting this degree I paid the bills by being a bike messenger, a cab driver, a waiter, and a bartender. Pedaling the streets of Chicago was a blast. The weather often sucked, but the thrill of weaving in and out of cabs and buses on a mountain bike was quite a kick. After knocking myself out on the asphalt on the corner of Jackson and Michigan and another time when I flew through the air over a Miata, I decided to move up the food chain to the secure confines of a roomy yellow cab.

Around that time my two crazy brothers moved to town, and we quickly figured out that Chicago was going to be a lot of fun. Chicagoans are good, down-to-earth people as compared to the New Jersey/New Yorkers we were used to. Most of the inhabitants on the near north side were recent college grad yuppies from one of the Midwestern universities or state school systems of Michigan, Wisconsin, Illinois, Minnesota, and Indiana. They were overall nice people from Midwestern America. They weren't world traveling fashion designers and play writers of New York, but rather they were good hearted bankers, commodity traders, accountants, teachers, social workers, and actuaries who knew how to have fun.

After three years of being a monk I was ready for a little fun. The past three years of seclusion and self-reflection enabled me to quash my desires enough that I wasn't afraid to plunge back into life and get lost in its allure. Actually, I felt like I could partake of the toys of the senses and enjoy them like never before primarily because, for the first time, I realized I didn't need them to be happy. Happiness and purpose now came from interacting with life and using that experience to progress toward enlightenment. I felt the three years of submerging myself in spiritual mediation had paid off. I had a goal. I knew what it was, and I knew what I needed to do to get there.

To a degree I felt I was going back out into the world enlightened. I know that sounds bold, but recall I have a different definition of being enlightened than most. I believe we become enlightened once we understand what the purpose of life is. Once we realize, not just academically but truly understand, that the purpose of life is to rid ourselves completely of our ego, then I believe we are enlightened. Are we liberated? No. Let's not get ahead of ourselves. We are still in the bad marriage with our ego. We still walk, talk, and think via our ego. We have a long way to go, but we know where we need to get. The enlightened are aware of the bad marriage. They are aware of their mission. Buddha, Christ, and many others became enlightened and used that enlightenment to become completely liberated. We can too.

179

Be careful not to assume enlightenment too soon. Our ego can understand what I am saying and would love to walk around claiming it is enlightened. The Chinese have a saying, "Those who know do not say; those who say do not know." An enlightened person not only knows the goal of distinguishing the ego but realizes it from a place of thinking outside of the ego. This is hard to explain. You must observe your ego from the "true" self. If we meditate on our ego long enough and begin to see its flaws and how it is our captor and the cause of our pain, there will come a time when we get disgusted enough and shun it just enough to find ourselves criticizing it from a slightly removed perspective.

At first this will be from the perspective of a more refined ego, which is actually criticizing the lesser, more obvious egotistical traits. If we continue to meditate upon discovering all the aspects of the ego, and we are willing to constantly assume our current heightened perspective is actually the ego simply evolving to a more refined persona, eventually we will see it as so separate a creature we will begin to stand separate. If we learn, even momentarily, to despise all aspects of our ego and are willing to admit we are still subjected to the ego and committed to its defeat because we realize it is the cause of all our unhappiness, then we can begin to identify with the "true self."

It is an important milestone on the path toward enlightenment when you discover a foundation of happiness which you experience simply because you are alive and because you realize you are on an amazing, unlimited path towards bliss. You will feel this joy simply because you know you are no longer fighting the river of life, which is trying to take you towards wisdom and enlightenment, but rather floating with it. Building a more complex ego, competing with others for comforts, trying to improve your ego's ability to acquire comforts are what the normal person does with his or her life and is in contradiction to the flow toward growth and the flow of life. You feel the joy of not caring what people think about you. You realize that fear of death, rejection, finances, etc. is unnecessary, and when you meditate upon that thought you feel moments of liberation from those constant subconscious burdens.

Lao Tzu, the founder of Taoism wrote in the *Tao Te Ching* that people must strive to attain the *wu wei*, which means "not forcing" or "to flow with" or "to do nothing" against the flow of life. Basically, he was saying that life is a struggle for most because they are moving against life's intention or flow. Life is trying to push us towards the destruction of our ego. The average person, he would say, is pushing back against this force. They are not moving toward the blissful existence that God sent us here to embody but rather they are busily forging the creation of the ego, refinement of that ego, and the pursuit of its desire. We are moving one way and life is moving the other. We are salmon swimming upstream. Lao Tzu is the guy on the inner tube with a cold drink and a smile, floating by us effortlessly with the current.

While in Chicago I would go out and drink booze with my friends and then not touch it for eight months. I was busy with school, work, and enjoying life. I stopped fearing what I was going to do, and I saw the utility in getting a career, experiencing life, and growing from life. I began to realize this was the playground of my ego, and this was a great place to observe and learn about it.

Jesus said "resist not evil" (Matthew 5:39). Why would he say such a scandalous statement? Because the truth of the matter is that there is no evil, only ignorance. I ran into a Hindu monk

182

one day, and we got into a discussion about spirituality. I mentioned something about "the evil temptations of life" and out of the corner of my eye I saw him grimace. I asked him why he made that face, and he smiled and said, "I hate it when I hear westerners say the word 'evil.' They are typically talking about something they don't understand. If you think something is evil, you will resist it. The more you resist or avoid something the less understanding you have regarding it. What happens if you change your language from 'the evil temptations of the world' to 'I am still ignorant as to why I have these worldly temptations.' Look what happens. You now changed it from something you should avoid, 'evil,' to something you should investigate thoroughly, 'ignorance,' so that you can gain the knowledge that will liberate you." In other words, "resist not evil." What you resist or fear you are always tied to. Once you become aware of its shortcomings and the unhappiness that attachment will bring you, you are free.

This is what my task in life was at this time. I did my three years of mediation to gain the enlightenment that my ego was the cause of my suffering and getting rid of it was my mission. Now I can go about my life and learn about my ego as it acts out its desires. Here I shall get close to the "evil" in an attempt to see the flaws in its logic. Once I truly see all its flaws my attachments to it will be over. For now, I must live with it.

I knew a lot more about my ego than I did before I went to the commune but by no means had control over it. Usually it would react, and I would have no idea. Sometimes it would react and I would figure it out several days later upon contemplation, and other times I would see it rear its ugly head right in front of me. But that would only happen if it was really egregious. The important thing was that I was observing and picking up bits and pieces.

We do not have to walk into a church, temple, or mosque in order to have a "religious" experience. A religious experience is any experience that helps us identify our ego, helps you realize its uselessness, and thereby enables you to take another step towards its defeat. It can and will happen anywhere. Just pay attention, and you will become aware of the destructive effects of the way you are living your life. At that moment you are in "God's house." God built the world for you to use to learn and grow. People built churches and temples, which are just pretty buildings where people go for many self-serving reasons (to feel good about themselves, to appear good to others, to placate their fear of dying, etc.). These are all acts which add to the ego. These are the acts that solidify our addiction to the ego. We may call these places "houses of God," but they are not houses of God if we are using them to become more self-righteous.

It reminds me of a story: There was once a woman who was religious and devout and filled with love for God. Each morning she would go to church. And on her way children would call out to her, beggars would accost her, but so immersed was she in her devotions that she did not even see them.

Now one day she walked down the street in her customary manner and arrived at the church just in time for service. She pushed the door, but it would not open. She pushed it again harder, and found the door was locked. Distressed at the thought that she would miss service for the first time in years and not knowing what to do, she looked up. And there, right before her face, she found a note pinned to the door.

It said, "I'm out there!"

We can have tremendous growing experiences in houses of worship, but not because somebody labeled them holy places. We can grow there because we are paying attention and are discovering our destructive habits and have decided to exchange them for less or non-destructive ways of seeking happiness. A church is a building, neither holy nor evil. It is just a building. What we do with our time in it is what is important. The main thing to remember is that we never walk out of the true "church," "temple," or whatever you want to call it. Life is our temple. We cannot hide from life's push, imploring, and desire to help us grow.

Chicago gave me many opportunities to learn. In the city, everyone is right on top of each other. There are many occasions to interact, especially as a cab driver, bartender, or waiter. You work with and meet many interesting people with very diverse and complicated personalities. You meet some humble people, but more often in a city you meet big, eccentric egos. They are very obvious and therefore make it easy to observe and learn from. The city is a harsh environment and therefore a harsh ego is needed to cope, or so we tell ourselves.

While I was learning about some of my ego's personality, I was also creating new personalities to suit my new environment. I typically wasn't aware of this, but that's how egos are normally created. The best experience I had in Chicago was meeting my first wife. She was attractive, funny, and had your typical array of issues as I did. I believe all couples are paired with an equal level of "maturity" regardless how more destructive one of the partners seems because that only means that the other partner is equally immature for putting up with it. There are no victims in most cases, minus the abused.

Our marriage was pretty typically dysfunctional. We had fun to a point and thought we loved each other. We were simply too young to know what we wanted in a relationship. She got bored, started sleeping around, I beat the guy up, we went to counseling, and a year later we divorced. All in three years.

Neither of us was fit for a happy marriage. She believed her pleasure came from men wanting her, and I was so egotistical that I thought I could be the source of her happiness. I thought that I could be her God and give her happiness where there wasn't any. This is just the way life is. This is how we learn. I had to understand that I created a personality that thought it would find happiness by trying to make other people happy. It made me feel good to be needed. It made me feel powerful, thinking I could give them happiness and, of course, take it away. They feared losing me, for a while, until they resented me for owning their happiness. My flaw was harder to see because I was "so nice" as I was slowly convincing you I am the source of your happiness. This put me in control. You can't leave your happiness nor upset it. This was how I controlled the people I believed I needed in my life for my happiness. But I seemed so selfless while I was doing it...sinisterly evil. And it worked for a long time until the affairs. Then it all came crashing down on us.

The pain is meant to help us grow. Why would we want to experience that pain again? The dull-witted thinks I just need a better spouse. The thoughtful want to know all the elements that caused the unhappy conclusion including, and this is that hard part, MY wrong ideas that were part of this ignorance.

Marriage is one of the greatest tools for learning. We can fool our friends for a long time and maybe forever, but our spouse will eventually see the real us. This is a tremendous gift. Marriage always works perfectly. It always reveals a more honest depiction of you. People divorce for many reasons. They may want out because the illusion is over and they want to go back into hiding. They believe leaving is easier than doing the work of changing. Some divorce because they are okay with growing and they realize that they married to cover up a fear (being alone, poverty, social acceptance, etc.) and that the emptiness of love in the marriage was more painful than the fear the union originally compensated for. Divorce is not morally wrong. Staying married is not morally right. Growing is morally right. Preventing growth in exchange for a moral construct (marriage, social acceptance), or out of fear (fear of condemnation, fear of being alone, fear of the unknown) is wrong.

I am not a supporter of a bad marriage. I am sorry, but I am a hopeless romantic for healthy relationships and not a fan of putting off happiness due to socially contrived commitments. We are here to find enlightenment not to be a martyr or a slave to social convention. That may offend some people, but I have come to realize that we will never do an injustice to anyone if we are striving to grow toward enlightenment. Typically we waste many years stuck in unhappy situations due to familial, social, religious, or financial brainwashing. We don't move on fast enough. I see a rise in divorce as a sign that people are not putting up with unsatisfying relationships. Of course, there are many people who are bailing on marriages because they are too lazy to do the work, but if they are that lazy, who wants to be married to them anyway? Your conviction and commitment should be towards growth and not humanly created obligations.

I was so happy to be out of that marriage. She grew tired of me owning her happiness, and I was exhausted of the constant work of convincing her I was her happiness. The relationship was perfect because we create the situation that taught us exactly what we needed to learn. That marriage happened because she was pretty, which my ego liked for social admiration and physical comfort, she had a lot more money than I did, which my ego liked for the ease it would bring to my financial struggles, and lastly she had the psychological makeup of someone who I could convince that she needed me. This gave me the security that I could control this thing that was serving my other needs. When you become aware of the way your ego thinks and acts, you will realize that the word "thing," which I just called my ex-wife, who is a wonderful human being, is an accurate description of how the ego thinks. It really doesn't care about them nor their happiness. Our ego will do things for our spouse which may appear selfless, but in reality, it only does them because it realizes it won't get to go play golf later if it doesn't watch the kids now. It's very businesslike. Not loving at all.

God Bless the Nemesis

A certain rabbi was adored by everyone in his community, who were all enchanted with everything he said. Apart from Isaac, that is, who never missed an opportunity to contradict the rabbi's interpretations and point out errors in his teaching. The others were disgusted by Isaac's behavior but could do nothing about it.

One day, Isaac died. During the funeral, the community noticed that the rabbi was looking very sad. 'Why so sad?' asked someone. 'He found fault with everything you did!'

'I'm not sad for my friend, who is now in heaven,' replied the rabbi. 'I am sad for myself. While you all revered me, he challenged me, and so I was forced to improve. Now that he's gone, I'm afraid I might stop growing.'

Author Unknown

CHAPTER SIXTEEN

How well do you know your ego? How do you discover it? How do you separate yourself from it permanently? Father DeMello used to say that he recommended meditation but found awareness more useful. Mediation, he would say, is like a spot light while awareness was more like a floodlight. Awareness is the ability to pay attention to your thoughts and actions and those of others. Awareness is simply being alert to all of life and all tricks of the ego. It seems simple, but most people are not willing to do it. We are all capable, but very few people have the "guts" to do it. We are afraid of what we might find. We are afraid we may feel obligated to fix a problem if we spot one, so we are better off keeping our head in the sand.

Some have said that the three most difficult things for a human being to do is to return love for hate, include the excluded, and to say we are sorry. How can this be? None of these acts take great physical strength nor great intellectual prowess. Yet almost nobody can do them. It's because the ego doesn't like these humble acts, and we are our ego. In this chapter I would like to discuss two things that will piss off your ego immensely. First, I want to reveal how dumb the ego is when it comes to finding happiness, and, second, I want to review how brainwashed we are by our ego's way of thinking.

How would you react if someone cut you in line? Cut you off in their car? Shoved you? Insulted you or a loved one? The examples of human hostility and stupidity are, I'm afraid, limitless. If you are anything like the average person, you will say, "I would become upset." Let me show you how completely insane that response is.

If you can walk away from this book with just one thing, please let it be this. People do not dictate how we react, but we do, and we typically pick the worst reaction. From now on I want you to say, "I chose to upset myself when that person did that." This is a more accurate description of what occurred. The person, who was a jerk, did something rude. Ask yourself, "Was it necessary for me to upset myself when they did that?" From birth we have been told the answer is "yes." This brainwashing, which I referred to earlier in the book as the crack we have all been injected with since birth, has told us we are not in control of our reaction and that we are powerless victims. We have been told it is "normal" to become upset when wronged by people. Therefore, we are stuck in a pattern of unhappiness, and we believe we are not in control.

How can we be in control of our happiness if any knucklehead can come along and upset us? Under this mentality we could be having a great day and be completely happy and ahead of us are 1,000 human interactions and each one has the ability to take our happiness away from us. Does this really make sense? Are we really forced to become upset?

Let me show you how stupid this is. Do you realize that not all people react the same way to the rudeness of another? The same person, typically, will be rude to dozens of different people in a single day and the recipients of that rudeness don't all experience the exact same level of "upsetness." Some become irate, some mad, and others mildly irritated. Why is this? What is the constant in this equation? The jerk being an ass to everyone. What is the variant in the equation? The recipients. So the power to dictate the reaction is actually in the recipient and not the abuser. Did you realize this? Did you realize that not only are you in control of your reaction but that you also have the option of not becoming upset at all?

Our ego hates this reality. It loves upsetting itself. It likes the thrill. The only thing it enjoys more is blaming someone else for causing it. The ego loves drama but hates taking responsibility for the drama, so it must blame someone else. Do you realize that if you explained this to 100 people, typically, all 100 of them would most likely say that it is "natural" to upset yourself upon being insulted or upon being confronted with rudeness?

Do you want to start taking control of your life? Do you want to start living life consciously? Do you want to liberate yourself from victimization? Do you want to liberate yourself from stupidity? Do you want to be in control of your happiness? Do you want to stop people from shitting all over your peaceful day? If so, think before you react. Cease the habit of compulsory reaction the type of reaction that lunges out of you unconsciously. Be in control. Hear how your ego wanted to react, and then think about why it wanted to react that way. Realize that a negative reaction is not necessary. Say, "I can choose not to upset myself," or better yet, "I can choose not to allow others to dictate how I should feel right now."

I know what you are thinking. This is not normal. This isn't human. It is not fair to let this jerk get away with this wrong. Shouldn't I react? You are correct. This is not the normal reaction, but it is a smarter/enlightened reaction. This certainly is human. If not having control of my happiness is human, then I would rather not be human. The third point is most interesting. Many people feel a reaction is necessary in order to exact justice.

Let me ask you several other questions. If you were walking down the road and saw a homeless, abused child, should you become upset by that? Should you feel proud about doing charity? Finally, and the one people like the least, should we feel good when someone compliments us? Almost all people answer all three of these questions with "yes." Would it shock you if the answer to all three is actually "no"? I know your ego is screaming objections. It hates not being in charge. It hates the idea of us taking away its power.

Let's take one at a time. You see a homeless child. Should it upset you? No! You, of course, are thinking how horribly

197

dispassionate I am. How depleted of feelings and compassion. All wrong. Does your reaction of upsetting yourself solve the child's problem? No. You can become as upset as you feel fit. That, of itself, does not feed the child, house the child, nor solve whatever myriad of other psychological, physiological, or intellectual problems the child may or may not have. Action will be required to assist the child. Did you find the assumption? You are assuming you need to upset yourself to be driven to do something. This is not the case!

Should we feel proud for doing charitable work? No. Is it really charitable if we did it in order to reward ourselves with pride? Did we do it for them or for us? It made us feel good to do the charity. Our ego did the charity to feel proud of itself, to be applauded by other egos, in order to be lifted in social admiration. There is no charity in that.

Should we feel good about compliments? No. Our ego is really going to hate this one. It loves to reward itself. It loves the accolades of other egos. It adores the red carpet, the humble acceptance speech. "Oh, please. Hold your applause." Bullshit. Did you ever consider the fact that if a compliment lifts you, the opposite must also occur? You will be depleted when the compliment doesn't come, or, worse, you will be dejected when criticized. This is all ego. This is all a waste of emotion. This is not human. This is subjecting yourself to a stupid emotional rollercoaster and every turn, dip, and rise is out of your control. You might as well be a monkey in a cage that waits to be fed, pet, punished, or rewarded and let your emotions rise and fall with each uncontrollable interaction.

Do you think your soul needs recognition? Do you think your soul would only help a needy child if it first upset itself? Do you think your soul needs to inflate itself with compliments or charity work? Do you think your soul experiences pride? Do you think your soul experiences the insults from an immature idiot? NO, NO, NO, NO, NO!

If you can understand that *you* are in control of your emotions and not others, you will jump light years ahead in your ability to map out your ego. Why, you may be asking. Let me ask you this: when are you better at analyzing a situation and objectively observing it? when you are upset or when you are unemotional about it? I'm assuming we all agree that we are all

199

better at analyzing a situation when we aren't upset. Being upset seems to push the analysis toward reducing our "upsetness" not towards truly understanding the situation. Can we agree on that?

If this is true and it is true that our best chance at understanding our ego is to observe it interacting in the world, then we will obviously be much better at it if we are not upset. Okay, that is the clinical justification, but for purely practical reasons why, *for the love of God*, are we all running around allowing idiots to make us upset? It's simply stupid.

I love the story Father DeMello used to tell. One day a guy was walking to work with a friend and they stopped to buy a newspaper from a sidewalk vendor. During the exchange the vendor said something rude to one of the men. When they walked away the friend said to the other guy, "Man, that guy was a jerk to you. Let's not stop there anymore."

The other guy responds, "Why should we let that guy dictate to us where we can stop to buy our newspaper?"

Isn't that beautiful? Why would I let that guy dictate how I am going to live my life? This man is liberated. He thinks for himself. His happiness is not at the whim of some jerk. He is in control of his life. He controls his happiness. He is enlightened.

How many people do you know can think this way? Do you know anyone? If you don't think this way, you are a passenger in a bumper car going through life. You are not in control of your physical or emotional course in life. You go where people tell you to go. You feel what they tell you to feel. You are like a monkey who screams every time someone pulls your tail. This is what happens when egos are in control. Somebody's ego pulls the tail of our ego, and there goes your bumper car careening off in a new direction chosen by some idiot your ego didn't like. Good grief...we are all a mess.

Let's get back to the poor homeless child you passed on the street. Is it necessary to become upset? No. Is it necessary to upset ourselves in order to feel motivated to do something to help this child? No. Becoming upset, as we discussed, only makes us less able to rationally assist them. We are blinded by our own selfish desire to relieve our upset-ness, and therefore we can't focus on the needs of the child.

People actually think that if I don't get upset I won't do anything to help someone in need. This is crazy. We can do something, and that which we decide to do will be what is best for them and not designed to relieve our upset-ness. This also goes for the guy who spit in your face. I know this is going to shock you, but you will be much smarter at dealing with that guy if you are not boiling over with anger. Even if you decide to punch him in the face, which may be the wisest reaction, do it because you thought clearly about what would be the proper thing to do objectively and not because you are trying to relieve your upset-ness. You, at least, must agree that walking around pissed off for a week because of that idiot is pretty stupid. Punch him and move on unattached, if you choose.

The most powerful teaching on this subject is found in the *Bhagavad Gita*. Some of you may know that the main setting is on a battlefield. Arjuna is the king and his cousin is coming with his army to take his kingdom. Arjuna was a spiritual person and tried to give his people a good, fair life. His cousin was a ruthless ruler that wanted his kingdom in order to amass more power and was not concerned about the quality of life for those subservient to him.

Arjuna, while climbing onto his chariot to lead his army out onto the field of battle, began to question the righteousness of his actions and in the battle in general. He began to think, "Should I kill? Is it right for me to go and kill in order to defend land, or a kingdom, myself, or my people? Can any violence be justified? When is my life more important than someone else's? Should a spiritual person shun all violence?"

If you can envision the chariots in that day, they typically had several horses harnessed to a small chariot with two wheels under a small platform for two people to stand on. One person would be controlling the reins to direct the horses while the other would engage in battle with a long spear and/or sword. Anyway, as Arjuna was preparing himself and having this internal moral debate about the righteousness of violence, his charioteer turned and began to urge him toward his duty to fight. What Arjuna did not realize was, as the story goes, the Lord Krishna had become his charioteer in order to give him the instruction on "proper action."

Krishna explained to Arjuna that it was his duty to fight. We all have a dharma, and that dharma is our duty in this life.

Arjuna, being a good and just king had a duty to his people to protect them from this aggressor who desired to take this kingdom and turn it into his selfish possession at the expense of the people who live in it. He would turn them into his slaves and attempt to wring every bit of life out of each and every one of them for his own selfish pleasure and wealth.

Just as it would be wrong for the monk to come down from the mountain to join this battle and to kill, it is equally wrong for Arjuna to run to the mountain to hide from this battle in order to avoid his duty to fight. Krishna then gave him one of the most valuable teachings ever explained to mortals, which we all need to hold dear and incorporate in our life. Krishna said, "Arjuna, plunge into the din of battle yet keep your heart at the lotus feet of the Lord."

This is it. This is the teaching that explains how to live life. This is the goal of each of us. This is living from the soul's perspective and not the ego's. The ego, in order to act, believes it must become upset. It must be offended. There must be a wrong for me to need to right. I must upset myself when offended or to act toward justice. This is all wrong.

204

Krishna explains that we can act while we keep our mind and heart at peace at the lotus feet of the Lord. Remember, do you make better choices about correcting a wrong when you are upset, mad, or frustrated or when your mind is clear and you are unaffected? Do you make better decisions when you are the one injured or when you are giving non-biased advice to a friend who is upset? The one with the clear mind makes better decisions about how to correct a wrong.

When you are upset your vision is blurred with anger, and, guess what, you aren't trying to correct a wrong in the universal sense, but rather you are trying to satisfy your anger or relieve your annoyance. You are trying to get relief, and therefore your reaction will be based on not what the person needs but rather the degree of your upset-ness. You are no longer trying to help that person but rather only trying to help yourself get over being mad, offended, or wronged. Your poor fragile ego. It needs to lash out. It needs to get its justice. As Buddha states, "You will not be punished for your anger; you will be punished by your anger."

205

This is going to sound horrible, but many people will give the homeless child money in order to relieve their own upset-ness. *They* will feel better about *themselves* if they give the kid money. Often people get mad when they believe someone else *makes* them uncomfortable. Have you ever found yourself mad at a sibling when they do something self-destructive? It's because we are mad that they *made* us worry about them. It is the same with the homeless child. Although you feel bad for them your ego is also mad that *they are forcing you* to deal with the harsh reality of life. Giving them a few dollars makes you feel like you are helping and thereby relieves you of that stress. Ask yourself, "Did you give them the money for them or for you or both?"

There is a lot of evidence that giving a homeless adult money won't help them. They will typically make bad decisions with that money. They will buy alcohol or drugs, which will further exacerbate their situation. It would be more helpful if you would fund a support program (shelter, counseling, food line, medical aid, etc.). But when we gave them the money we may not have been thinking clearly. We may have been trying to relieve our pain, our discomfort. We may have been blinded to their needs because we couldn't see past ours.

It's the same with all of life. When our spouse is upsetting us, we don't give them the advice they need for their objective growth. We give them the advice that will make them stop irritating us or will motivate them to give us what we want from them. Of course, we now know they never did irritate us but rather acted and we decided to upset ourselves. Either way, watch what the ego does in each of these scenarios. It is disgusting. It is completely self-serving. If you are willing and able to honestly see who you are when you identify with the ego, you should be disgusted and rightfully so. And thank God because that is the wisdom that will lead you toward liberation.

Have you spent your life honoring the needs of your ego or your soul? Are you in control of your reactions and thereby your life, or is your ego in control? The next time someone insults you watch your ego become upset and then, maybe for the first time, you have stepped out of your ego. You saw it for what it was. You separated yourself. You started the road toward liberation. You have become enlightened but not liberated. Let's not get ahead of ourselves, but you are now on the road towards complete liberation, Nirvana. Bliss. You now know what God wants you to do with this life.

Did They Hurt You or Did You Hurt Yourself?

Buddha seemed quite unruffled by the insults hurled at him by a visitor. When his disciples later asked him what the secret of his serenity was, he said:

"Imagine what would happen if someone placed an offering before you and you did not pick it up. Or someone sent you a letter that you refused to open; you would be unaffected by its contents, would you not? Do this each time you are abused, and you will not lose your serenity."

Teachings of Father Anthony DeMello

CHAPTER SEVENTEEN

Another major life changing event happened in 1993 when I was bartending at a charity dinner at the Museum of Natural History in Chicago. An elderly priest came up to my bar and we started to chat. He asked me what I wanted to be when I grew up, and I told him I was in my last year of finishing my Religious Studies degree and I was thinking about going to grad school to become a religion professor. He didn't seem very impressed. He asked me what I wanted to "accomplish" with my life. I said I am interested in religion, education, social change etc. I told him I wanted to do some small part to change the world. He smiled and said, "Listen kid, you're not gonna change diddly squat teaching religion to a bunch of snooty college kids who are only taking your stupid class because its either required or they thought it would be easier than Sociology 100. Your class will be filled primarily with kids who don't give a crap about religion and a handful of fundamentalist who you will want to strangle. You're gonna hate it after awhile."

To that I said, "Wow, dude, you are really depressing me."

He said, "I have a doctorate in religion and used to teach these punks. I also have a doctorate in psychology and a law degree. The law degree is what you are looking for. You don't really sound like you know what you want to do. With a law degree you can be a very effective activist for social issues, you can change laws through political involvement, or you can do many other things. You will always have religion in your private life, but making a career out of it is messy and limiting. Grab me another gin and tonic in a plastic cup so I can get out of this boring dinner. Nice meeting you kid, good luck."

I started law school the next fall. I graduated from law school in 1998 from the University of Denver. I found a small firm in the suburbs and began practicing civil rights law. We sued companies for sexual harassment, gender, age, race, disability and other types of discrimination. It was very rewarding work, and I worked with very intelligent, conscientious attorneys. I met very well intending students of law and attorneys. They aren't all blood sucking parasites. Not unless they are suing you, of course.

Law school and the practice of law made me mature intellectually and emotionally. Anything difficult can help you build the mental and emotion discipline you will need for self-analysis. In addition, it taught me a lot about the human condition. The study of law is really the study of human morals. Laws are the outcome of social debate over right and wrong. Our current social construct is the evolution of humanity's attempt to make life fairer, more secure, with a degree of self-serving properties for the historically social elite.

Education in general empowers us to defeat the ego by rooting out myth, moral constructs, and superstitions, and challenges our views by the confrontation of other views. Equally as important is that education helps you lose the fear that others must know more than you and that you are somehow at a disadvantage. I know this may seem petty but remember it is the ego we are combating and that silly, meager creature will design personality traits and crazy conspiracy theories to make it feel empowered over things it doesn't understand. In the absence of education we can convince ourselves of many crazy ideas. Just look to the millions of uneducated people around the world easily convinced that Americans "are the devil." They are at the whim of opportunists with their own hopes for power and fame looking for followers and soldiers to do their dirty work.

At this point in my life I enjoyed working at the firm litigating civil rights claims. Sunday through Thursday I would work hard, pray, and meditate and try to observe my egotistical attachments. On the weekends I would get drunk with my friends, mountain bike, run, and basically goof off. I was dating, but I was resolved to remain single for the rest of my life rather than get back into a marriage like the last one or for some other stupid reason I was yet unaware was lurking within me. I was pretty convinced I would remain single forever, and that was fine with me. I was able to conquer the part of my ego that was afraid of being alone. In addition, I lost the desire to fulfill a stereotypical life with a wife and kids in a house in the suburbs. I had no attachment to these social ideals. I had, gratefully, come to a place where I could choose a mate because it was fun and healthy for both of us. I wasn't attached to my career, my belongings, or to any particular future.

At the same time I began to grow more and more interested in analyzing the spiritual path. Although I have always been trying to pay attention and observe my ego, I realized I hadn't had the time or energy to make it my primary focus since leaving the commune. I was consumed by moving to the big city, financial survival, undergrad, a failed marriage, law school and practicing law, etc. There wasn't much time to take in everything I had been through. But after a few years as an attorney, life was becoming a bit more manageable, and I realized I was hungry to get my mind back on spiritual concepts and my growth in particular.

It was July 2000, and I was in Montana visiting the family. At this point my mother, three sisters and their families all lived in Bozeman, so it had become our family holiday gathering place since the late 1980's. While visiting, I decided to stop by the commune to see if any old friends were around and to enjoy sitting with the group in prayer. I lost touch with the commune when I left in 1990 but thought it would be nice to stop by. While I was there talking to an old friend, he introduced me to his step-daughter who happened to be the most beautiful woman I have ever seen. We talked for a little while and decided to go listen to a lecture together. I remember thinking how comfortable I was with her. This was unusual because typically my ego would get pretty nervous around such a beautiful woman. For whatever reason I immediately felt very "at home" with her. I didn't read much into it since I was living 900 miles away in Denver. I just thought it strange and was hoping it was another step in the death of my ego and its fear of aloneness or desire to possess.

The next day something occurred which seemed extremely minor at the time but turned out to be monumental. On July 4th I was barbequing with family and friends at a park in Bozeman, MT. My brother's pretty ex-girlfriend was there with her baby, and she told me that her and her husband just split up. I quickly started my typical "harmless" flirting, which I always did when a single, attractive woman was around. Although I was generally opposed to marriage at this point I was not opposed to sex. Even if I didn't intend on trying to have sex with the girl, I would still flirt with them. It was my "habit" to flirt. It is what my ego did to amuse itself. I had very little control over it. If there was a single pretty girl around, my ego took over and I "couldn't" control it. I was flirting with her before I realized I was doing it. This is how life is when the ego is in charge. We react before we have time to even think about why we are doing it.

While I was standing there flirting with this girl, I noticed my sister struggling with her two-year-old who was climbing on her while she was trying to change the diaper on her fussy six-month-old who was reaching for her to pick him up. I briefly thought, "I should go help her and pick that poor kid up." But, instead, I went back to flirting with this girl and even took her baby from her to pretend I was interested in her kid hoping she would fall for my tricks and give me the attention I wanted. I didn't even think our flirting would amount to anything. I just did it because it pleased "me" to garner attention for the moment.

The next day I was driving back to Denver on a pretty sunny day, and I threw in a tape of *bhajans* which, you may recall, are Hindu chants or prayers. While doing the chants I was thinking about my trip, and at this point in my life I was becoming pretty good at analyzing things I did and said but only after the fact. Sometimes I could catch it while I was saying it, but at this point I had a good habit of analyzing my ego and its silly interactions after the fact. It was like watching a really pathetic, immature movie.

215

During my review of the trip I came up to the moment when I looked over at my nephew crying on the blanket and reaching for someone to pick him up, and then I saw my reaction of momentary concern and return to my flirting. I would review situations from the perspective of a third person and analyze the motivation of my ego. I would watch each scene and ask, what childish reaction from others was I pursuing? What shallow satisfaction was my ego trying to experience? Etc.

When I saw the baby wanting comfort and me ignoring it and then grabbing the girl's kid from her that I was flirting with even though that kid was perfectly content where he was, it blew me away. The degree of my pettiness shocked me. The blatantness of the childishness I allowed within me sickened me. I was so sickened by myself that I pushed away from *it*, from *me*. I pushed so hard I broke free.

For the first time in my life I was so sick of my petty, self-serving egotistical ways that I really didn't want to experience it anymore. And like the snap of my fingers, my ego and all its parts sat in front of me with just enough distance that for the first time since the vision in the woods eleven years earlier, I saw it. It wasn't

216

the same monstrous redneck it once was. It had evolved into a suit and a briefcase. It was more sophisticated and less obviously awful. I wasn't shocked by its appearance. I knew most of the traits it portrayed. That last ten years of paying attention helped me become aware of it while I lived with it, used it, and added to it.

As I sat there driving eighty-five miles per hour south on Interstate 25 through Wyoming with the sun setting over the mountains and the endless plains of Wyoming, a little golden image appeared far off in the distance and was rapidly moving towards me. As it got closer it looked like the statue of Gautama Buddha I had seen so many times with closed eyes and that peaceful look of bliss on its face. As it got closer it was something I was not prepared for. It was the statue of Buddha, but his eyes were open, and he was smiling. He stopped right in front of me, and I began to beam with an amazing sense of joy and bliss. That ego I was just observing at a short distance felt a million miles away. I never experienced such bliss or peace. I didn't even feel like I had a body. I was in such bliss I began to worry that it would end, and to this reaction Buddha smiled and said, "That won't help." And by that I knew he meant fear is the problem. You

217

cannot hold onto bliss by fearing it will leave. I realized that I was not causing this experience but due to my disgust of my ego I was able to push my ego away enough for Buddha to help me obtain this bliss. I knew he did it to show me what else was possible and what I need to strive for on my own. I was ripped free from my ego. I felt, for the first time, full liberation. I could see my ego at a distance, I could feel its fears, wants, and desires, but it was separated from me. I was still driving and Buddha stayed in my sight the entire time for the next five or six hours.

When I got back to my apartment in Denver I kept trying to hold onto this vision as Buddha stayed with me. I kept chanting the *bhajans* as I sat on my bed. I had been chanting the same bhajan for approximately six hours. I was holding on to that feeling of bliss for dear life. I felt my old mentality, my current conglomerate of ego, trying to come back to roost. All through my struggle to hang on, Buddha just sat there smiling at me with that amazingly blissful grin. He seemed to be as happy to see me get there as I was, if that makes any sense from a being that is always happy. I sat on my bed afraid to go asleep. I was convinced that when I awoke it would all would be over and I would spend the

218

rest of my life trying to replicate this experience. Eventually, I drifted off to sleep.

In the morning I awoke but my sleep felt like it was for a minute. I sat up quickly and started to do the *bhajans* again, and I immediately felt like I was drifting away from the busy chatter of my mind once again. I began to drift away to a peaceful place of observation. I began to say to myself, "Don't fight it. Just don't associate with the chatter. Be the expansive sky and let the chatter be the drifting clouds." This is the image I was holding onto while I continued my *bhajans*. It is a very powerful mediation. Imagine that you are the blue, peaceful sky and let your thoughts float by as clouds. This separation from your thoughts helps you establish a distance from your ego.

After a while I walked to the bathroom and got in the shower. I stood under the hot water and continued my *bhajans*, and I began to become more and more comfortable with being the non-attached observer of my ego conglomerate. I could see my ego below me wondering what its day would be like back at the law firm, planning its agenda, discussing this spiritual experience with my friends, saying how wise it is and how wonderfully spiritual it is, that it is able to experience such bliss and how the world will be so impressed when he tells about his great feat, blah, blah, blah.

While this pathetic little man slathered itself with accolades, I sat silent, detached and neither tried to argue with it, shun it, criticize it, nor in any other way engaged in its banter. I just let it talk while I sat unattached and unaffected by its discussion. The longer I remained unattached the softer the voice got and further I seemed to drift from it, and then suddenly, SNAP, it was gone, and I found myself in a timeless state of bliss. I entered timelessness.

While standing there I realized the entire concept of time was created by our process of desire and satisfaction. We need time in order to experience the linear experience of "desire it, pursue it, get it, and try to hold onto it." We put ourselves in time, and we have the power to take ourselves back out of time, out of birth, out of death and the cycle of *samsara*, which Buddha described as the cycle of birth, decay, death, and reincarnation.

Timelessness occurs when you cease to want or to be attached to anything. The entire emotion of wanting is no longer an emotion you possess. This can occur when you become aware that the very act of wanting brings suffering. Focus on the suffering, and you will eventually reject the cause of suffering which is desire. Reject all desire, and you will be freed of suffering, and you will become liberated in timeless bliss.

You've Already Lost That Which You Hang On To

During the civil wars in feudal Japan, an invading army would quickly sweep into a town and take control. In one village, everyone fled just before the army arrived – everyone except the Zen master.

Curious about this old fellow, the general went to the temple to see for himself what kind of man this master was. When he wasn't treated with the deference and submissiveness to which he was accustomed, the general burst into anger.

"You fool," he shouted as he reached for his sword, "Don't you realize you are standing before a man who could run you through without blinking an eye!"

But despite the threat, the master seemed unmoved.

"And do you realize," the master replied calmly, "that you are standing before a man who can be run through without blinking an eye?"

Author Unknown

CHAPTER EIGHTEEN

The meaning of life can also be summed up as the pursuit of perfect happiness. Contrary to popular belief, "liberation" is not reached through a life of rigid discipline, abstention, or self-denial. It is attained through quite the opposite approach. Enlightenment is obtained through "selfishly" engrossing yourself in the pursuit of happiness. I say "selfishly" because liberation is done via the understanding of self and the ego's effect on self. As many have instructed us, "Man, know thyself." (Psalm 77:6) Liberation is accomplished via the study of self and then realization that the ego is a bad influence on the self that must be plucked out. For now, view the meaning of life as the art of becoming happier. It truly is that simple.

The pursuit of happiness is the key. Through evolving our understanding of happiness we will voluntarily surrender our ego, epitomize selflessness, and reach full liberation. This may seem completely contrary to what you think the spiritual path requires, but it isn't. Many people avoid the spiritual path because they, *wrongly*, believe, which I once did, that it is a path of sacrifice and abstaining from the things and experiences that bring us happiness. This couldn't be further from the truth.

Enlightenment is a shift from happiness as experienced by the ego, which will always be blanketed with fear and anxiety, to happiness as experienced without the ego, which has no negative repercussion and no limits. It is the evolution of happiness with lots of negative side effects (fear of loss) to bliss with no negative side effects. The voice telling you this will be a passionless path and a life of going without is your ego. Its broken and failed way of finding happiness is the only thing in jeopardy. A truer happiness without negative repercussions is what we will replace it with.

It can be said that liberation can only be reached through the pursuit of happiness because humans are not capable of any other pursuit. We have no other craving but happiness. Even the most uncomfortable act (emotional or physical) is done because we believe our happiness depends on it. We will be mean to loved ones because they threatened our emotional security, and it makes us feel better to "defend" ourselves or try and manipulate them back to a position that pleases us. We will endure physical challenges to impress, to make ourselves feel good about ourselves both emotionally and to satisfy physical vanity, or simply to feel good and healthy. All the above reasons make us feel good and therefore happy. There are even times when we convince ourselves that we did something selfless in order to help someone else, but in truth we did it because it made us feel good. This was discussed earlier regarding charitable acts.

If we are to "grow," we must first realize that all existence is dictated by our understanding of "happiness." The pursuit of happiness is the foundation of the human psyche. If we could remove every thought within our mind, starting from the most superficial concerns on down to the most foundational, we would arrive at the final statement that defines us: "WHAT WILL MAKE ME HAPPY?" The only difference between a "lesser" evolved ego and a "greater" evolved ego is the distance into the future it is able to consider the current decision's ramifications when making our present analysis of What Will Make Me Happy? The final destination of this evolution is to the soul's understanding that I need nothing in order to be happy.

225

"What will make me happy" is the statement that airs continuously as the foundation of our thought. It runs reel to reel without pause. We never reach for a glass of water, go to the bathroom, have sex, get out of bed, and even go to a shitty job (I'll explain) unless we conclude at that moment that it will make us happy. Every action taken is because that act answered the question, what will make me happy? At every moment in life we have a multitude of possible ways of expressing ourselves. We can say anything and express any of thousands of different physical expressions at each moment. The reason why you are reading right now is because out of those thousands of different possible expressions, reading is the option that, you believe, will make you most happy. Attempt to challenge this theory. It is ALWAYS the case. And I am well aware of the dangers of saying *always*. As Buddha stated, "There is no path to happiness: happiness is the path."

The obvious example, out of all the possible expressions, is when you are hungry: you typically pick eating because to eat something that taste good and to satiate that sensation of hunger is pleasing. It makes you happy. A more difficult or subtle example is going to work on Monday morning. One of many possible options is to stay in that nice, warm, cozy bed. But instead you get up, put on uncomfortable business attire, deal with traffic, and then work for eight to ten hours. Typically, at 6:00 am Monday morning you would think the option of staying in bed would make most people the happiest. Yet, every Monday morning millions of people choose the "less pleasing" expression of going to work. Ah ha, you say, your theory is bunk. But the truth of the matter is that getting out of bed on that cold Monday morning is the expression that would please us the most.

At that moment, while the alarm is blaring, you realize that if you do not get up and go to work, you will lose your job, and then your house and, soon after, most of the other things which also make you happy. Hence, getting out of bed, although at the moment seems less attractive than staying in bed, is the expression or act which will please us the most.

You must realize that this more "responsible" understanding of our happiness not only makes us happier in the long run, but it even makes us happier at that very moment. The sense of relief that you are not doing something self-destructive but instead doing what you know "you should be doing" is a sense of gratification that will make you happier than enduring the anxiety of not doing what you think you should be doing. Everyone is the same way. We are all hard-wired to seek happiness. The only difference between a drug addict and a "well-functioning" person is their ability to calculate all the repercussions of their actions. The question that motivates us is the same: "What will make us happy?"

A drug addict is so committed to immediate gratification that they fail to factor in the long-term negative repercussions of abuse. The happily married, well employed, financially secure individual has the ability to put off immediate gratification a million times in order to study for exams, complete college, do the dishes, take family trips to Disney World (which no "normal" adult really enjoys except my wife) save money for retirement, etc. Happiness is the progressive reward that coincides with our progress along the spiritual path.

I bring up this fundamental truth because I want people to embrace the path toward liberation. I do not want you to fear it as some intimidating undertaking that will disrupt your life and your happiness. It is the opposite. The path toward liberation is simply an awareness and analytical understanding, and thereby improvement, of your existing happiness. Build upon what you have. Improve what you have constructed. Enjoy the dropping of those ideas that obstruct your happiness and the fruits of a better happiness that makes life more enjoyable. Do not beat yourself up once you see a silly egotistical attachment. Instead, laugh at it and be happy you saw it. Drop it and move on.

At some point, and I do not expect you to think this way right away, there will come a time when you will look forward to people laughing at you. You will look forward to "embarrassing" yourself. You will look forward to having your feelings hurt. You will get a rush out of experiencing fear. You will realize what a gift these experiences are. You will watch your ego freak out and then realize that you are becoming the observer. You will begin to see your ego acting like a spoiled little child who became embarrassed, hurt, and was afraid. You will get a glimpse of life without those reactions and those harmful and unnecessary feelings. Where you once only experienced pain you will now experience the pain at a distance and beautiful liberation as you begin to feel what life can be like without fear. You will be experiencing what life is really meant to be. You will be doing what "God" has put you here to do. You will be using life to become liberated.

Happiness Leads to Liberation

A believer approached Rabbi Moche of Kobryn and asked: 'How should I best use my days so that God will be contented with my actions?'

'There is only one possible option: to live with love,' replied the Rabbi.

Minutes later, another follower approached him and asked the same question.

'There is only one possible option: try to live with joy.'

The first follower was taken aback. 'But the advice you gave me was different!'

'Not at all,' said the rabbi. 'It was exactly the same.'

Teachings of Father Anthony DeMello

CHAPTER NINETEEN

While standing in the shower enjoying my timeless state, I began to wonder what the rest of my life was going to be like. What kind of life does someone live if you have no desires or needs? I felt completely fearless. I understood the wandering mendicant who would just walk out towards life with no fear, no desires, and no needs. What would I do? I have a job at a law firm but no attachment to it. I have no family relying on me for income, and I don't care or have a need for anything not even a roof over my head. I felt like I could just start walking down the road with a smile on my face and not a care in the world. I would just walk with no destination or objective other than enjoying being alive.

Not caring what I did I eventually decided I might as well just continue doing what I have been doing. So I went to the office to see what would happen. At first I wondered how I would be received, walking around my law firm with a goofy look of bliss on my face. Attorneys don't do that. If you don't look incredibly busy and completely stressed out you are obviously goofing off and need more work. If I were my boss, I would assume I was on drugs. Well, I didn't make it that far.

Upon getting to my desk I opened a file of a client who was in prison and who had claimed he was abused by a prison guard. It was a pro bono (free representation for the "public good") case that my firm asked me to take on behalf of the firm (I told you they were nice people). I read the first page in the file a dozen times and realized I wasn't paying attention. I couldn't, nor did I want to, wrestle my mind away from the new found non-attached bliss I was experiencing. I began to wonder, "How am I going to be interested in the mundane ever again? How am I going to sit through weeks of trial preparation and the hundreds of hours combing through documents to find the 'smoking gun' that will win the case which was brought on behalf of my client who only brought the claim because someone offended his ego? Will I really be able to focus on a level necessary to be good at this, which is only fair to my client? The answer was so obviously, "no," that it was laughable. Apparently, this law thing wasn't going to work.

I thought, I have been trying all my life to get to this blissful place, and I'm not going to give it up because it interferes with my job, even if I did just borrow $120,000.00 to get this degree. Enlightenment is a little more valuable to me.

I began to think about what I should do. Then I thought, "Hey what about the cult? They wouldn't mind me walking around with this goofy look on my face without a care in the world. They would probably even give me room and board so I don't have to live on a park bench in Denver." So I picked up the phone, called the commune, they put me through to Human Resources, and the woman on the other end of the phone remembered me. I asked her if she had any jobs I could take. I told her I would do anything: construction, wash dishes, yard work, teach...anything. She responded, "Aren't you an attorney?"

To which I replied, "Yes."

She said, "Well, our attorney quit last week, and we are desperate for a new one."

I said, "I'll wrap things up here at the firm and come up as soon as possible." I went into my boss' office and told her that I was giving my notice so I could finish writing a book I started. This was easier to explain than the truth. She asked how much time I could give her to wrap up my files and I answered as long as it takes. She seemed relieved.

During the following two weeks I spent my nights talking to Buddha, doing many hours of *Bhajans* and prayers and walking around Denver in a blissful stupor. At work everything miraculously came into its place. Half of the cases I had mysteriously settled and the other half seemed to fall into long term delays where nothing had to be done for a while. It all happened within a week. It was a miracle.

The commune called and asked if I could come to Montana in two weeks so the Board of Directors and Executive Team could interview me. At this point, I had already quit my job at the firm without having the job at the commune, but I didn't care. As I got off the phone with the commune the senior partner that I worked with walked into my office and asked how everything was going. I gave her an update of all my cases and we concluded that I could leave at any time. I came in one more day to organize, clean up, and say goodbye.

In July 2000, I arrived at the commune. I was still living in my blissful state. I met with the Board and Officers, and they offered me a job. It didn't pay that well and would not leave me much to live on after my $800 a month student loan payment, but I didn't care. My first day at the commune I awoke, went to that same metal building I started this journey in back in 1988, and engaged in morning prayer. It was strange yet wonderful to be back.

The commune was quite different now. The woman who was the charismatic leader/guru was gone and being treated for advanced Alzheimer's. With her departure the commune went through a difficult couple of years of political, theological, and leadership instability. They also experienced hard financial times. Many of the longtime members had left the organization and the resident count went from 700 when I was there in the late 1980s to 50 or so people in 2000. The commune was basically focused on disseminating the writings of the former leader and serving current members of the church worldwide, which held steady in the U.S. but had grown rapidly in Russia and South America. They estimated their numbers to be in the tens of thousands worldwide.

I settled into my office and began to familiarize myself with the church's legal issues and overall current state of affairs. The job entailed negotiating cattle grazing leases, hunting leases, employment issues, housing issues, liability issues and a plethora of land and environmental issues as you can imagine come with managing a 33,000-acre ranch.

As with my job at the firm, it was difficult for me to engage myself with all the legal issues at the church and found myself far more interested in the evolution of the theological interpretation and the debate that had been ongoing since the "guru" left. With the teacher gone the different factions of students began arguing for their interpretation of how the teachings should be interpreted, who should interpret, what qualifies as interpreting vs. just policy making. They argued over questions such as should rituals be allowed to evolve as they had under the guru, or should they be frozen in time as expressed at her departure? These were fascinating questions, and I wholeheartedly thrust myself into the debate to the consternation of the Board of Directors and Executive Team.

Each morning I would go to prayer, go for a run, have breakfast and then go to the office. Even though I came here to selfishly hide in my own bliss, I quickly realized that the church had many legal, financial, and theological issues to grapple with, and I wanted to help. I was kind of hoping that if I could get some of the legal stuff resolved, I could find time to create a teaching position and try to teach some of the helpful things I learned over the years about the path which, to be honest, I felt their teachings lacked.

One of my main contentions with their orthopraxy (right practice), was the fact that they thought "resist evil" was the proper teaching. I felt this teaching was severely holding back the growth of their members. They encouraged people to live in fear and ignorance. Like the Hindu monk explained to me many years earlier, don't look at your attachments as evil but rather as ignorance. If you believe you are ignorant, you will rush in, investigate, and thereby eventually get over your ignorance. You will become wise to the fact that it was your ignorant belief that the act or thing had power over you. Alcohol isn't innately "bad." Can you develop an unhealthy attachment to it? YES. But don't blame the object. That is just stupid. Empower yourself by

238

realizing that nothing is stronger than you. If you have a weakness, it is in your wrong belief and wrong attachment not the object of your desire. If you view your ignorance as evil, you will avoid them and your ignorance will persist.

I realize there is a time for abstention. I spent many years abstaining which gave me the ability to clear my mind and step away from the blinding desire that dictated my thoughts, and that abstention gave me time to realize the basic truth, "That all attachment is the cause of all suffering." Not the act nor the object nor the person but my attachment to it/them caused me to suffer. My lack of realization that every "need" comes with suffering, wanting, fear of losing, and the angst of knowing at death all I covet will be lost was what was holding me back from bliss. It was not some "evil" external force.

About six weeks into my new position I went by the house of that old friend I knew from my earlier days at the commune. To my delight his step-daughter was visiting. She is the one I ran into a few months back when I stopped by the commune during one of their conferences. I think he said it was his step-daughter, but I'm not sure because when I saw her he became so irrelevant that I couldn't really hear him anymore. Her beauty was so mesmerizing I couldn't listen to his Scottish accented baloney at that moment. I was lost in her. We talked, and she told me of her plans of moving to Phoenix in the very near future to go to school for interior design. I was not happy to hear she was leaving, but at the same time I was fine with it. I was still of the mentality that life would work itself out, so I thought I would hang out with her until she left town.

Within six weeks I was so in love with her I knew we would be together for the rest of our lives. The relationship was so easy to be in it was effortless fun and pure enjoyment. I had no fear of it ending, I never felt a need to impress her, and I didn't feel any need to be anyone other than who I was. I began to realize what love was like when you don't fear the loss of it. It is truly amazing and effortless. Obviously the sex is amazing also. No inhibitions, no fear, true pleasure. Thank God I was far enough along on the path towards conquering my fears and attachments that when this amazing woman came along I didn't freak out and lose her. It was the strangest thing. I knew she was by far the nicest, happiest, prettiest person I have ever met, and normally you would really want to possess and therefore act like you really want to possess and smother the entire experience (*"Don't crush the bunny Lenny."*) ...I saw all of these qualities and knew I would enjoy having her in my life, but at the same time I realized my happiness didn't depend on it. Life would be great with her, but it would also be great without her. I didn't need her for my happiness. I could find great happiness with her, but my happiness didn't require her presence. Imagine how well you can enjoy someone's company when you don't fear, at all, losing them. Unqualified love is another beautiful benefit about surrendering the ego. In the next chapter I will explain this further. The effect is mind-blowing.

My hopes of teaching at the church never happened. The damn "cult" fired me after six months for "insubordination." Man, this was the third time I'd been rejected by the same cult. That has to be a first! The problems between me and the powers-that-be at the church were born out of fundamental differences of how to manage someone's spiritual path. The church leaders, I felt, were earnestly trying to preserve a photograph of the teachings as left to them from the guru. Whenever someone applied the teachings or ritual in a way they felt was contrary to the photograph in their head, they would step in and implore a different route. If that didn't work, they would argue for a different route, and if that didn't work, claim it violated the church belief system and prohibit it. I believe their intentions were good, but that is not enough of a qualification to assume the role of spiritual teacher.

If you have not conquered enough of your ego in order to realize when you are simply imposing your views on the rest of the world, then don't try to teach. Step back, work on your own stuff and let God, via the rules already in place in life, teach. Let trial and error and life's happiness and sorrow lead people to enlightenment. Encourage the study of those writings and teachings of the enlightened that seem to be the least altered over the years, and then leave them to their own interpretation and judgment. Practicing your own judgment over your path is essential. If you want to sit in a church and have the "truth" told to you, then you will probably be sitting in that same pew in the next life asking the same questions and live a very similar life again.

In addition, the church leaders took great offense to my philosophy that at some point a student must engaging in "forbidden acts." By this I mean they must confront their attachments. The commune taught that alcohol, pre-marital sex, rock music, certain decadent foods, certain colors, and a myriad of other activities were all "bad" or evil influences that needed to be avoided if you were to become enlightened. I argued that they were not evil but rather simply objects and acts. I argued they had no inherent power over people but rather that the problem was people's attachment to the object and activity.

I felt they needed to embrace Christ's teaching of "resist not evil." Don't avoid what you are ignorant about. Rush in, wisely, and observe, learn and overcome your ignorant attachments. They were encouraging abstention and weakness in the presence of the very attachments their students needed to transcend.

So the cult fired me. Of course, I'm joking when I call this place a "cult." There really isn't a good definition of a "cult." It is typically just used as derogatory slang in order to discredit a religion you either don't like or don't understand. The commune was a great place in some ways, but in other ways it was pretty messed up. Either way, it was an extremely important part of my spiritual path and gave me most of the tools and concepts I needed and, for that, it will always have a fond place within me.

After getting let go by the commune I asked Azure, the hot chick I talked about earlier, what she wanted to do and I would do it with her. She was twenty-five at the time, and I was thirty-three. She spent her youth in California, Florida, and rural Colorado but had been in Montana since age sixteen. I could tell she wanted to do some exploring. I didn't have much to offer financially, but I could tell she didn't care. She was very independent, the oldest of nine siblings and knew how to take care of herself. We decided to take a road trip down the California Coast and to visit some friends in Portland, San Francisco, and Los Angeles. I told her I was going to try and write a book about my quest for enlightenment while trying to find a job. We spent the next couple of weeks driving down the California coast, playing and visiting friends. Azure decided that she wanted to move to Los Angeles. Although I wasn't licensed to practice law in California I knew it would work out, so we went back to Montana, packed up her nice stuff, threw my crappy belongings in the trash, and off we went.

Right Practice

When the Zen spiritual teacher and his disciples began their evening meditation, the cat who lived in the monastery made such noise that it distracted them. So the teacher ordered that the cat be tied up during the evening practice. Years later, when the teacher died, the cat continued to be tied up during the meditation session. And when the cat eventually died, another cat was brought to the monastery and tied up.

Centuries later, learned descendants of the spiritual teacher wrote scholarly treatises about the religious significance of tying up a cat for meditation practice.

Unknown Author

CHAPTER TWENTY

I have not been very flattering to either mainstream religion or the practice of psychology in this book. Let me set the record straight. I actually think both institutions serve a great purpose in society. Psychology is more honest about what it is trying to accomplish, so it isn't fair to group the two together. Psychologists seem to be trying to assist people in finding happiness by assisting them in building a stronger ego and thereby helping them cope in the world of egos. Religion, on the other hand, is not so "honest." It claims to be advocating the teachings of Jesus, Buddha, and/or the other prophets, but they simply are not. They are not encouraging enlightenment but rather fear pacification. Let's be honest, your average person belongs to a religious sect in order to pacify their fear of death, to feel like they are being a good person, to be judged well in the eyes of their peers, to feel superior, to feel protected by some divine source, or for some other bullshit reason that makes them feel good about themselves. This is all rubbish.

246

Christ did not come to make peace but rather to rock your world with the truth that will act like a sword and liberate you from your ego. Religion isn't teaching this. Religion is run by a bunch of egos who want to wear pretty robes and stand before you and feel the power of your belief that they are the mediator between you and God. We know it's crap, but we act like we believe it because we don't know why we are here and they are the only ones claiming to have the answer. Well, either they do know the meaning of life and they aren't telling us, or they don't know and made up this dogmatic bullshit in order to get our admiration. It was exactly the same in Jesus's day. In Matthew 22:15, Jesus states, "Woe to you, scribes and Pharisees, hypocrites! Because ye shut up the kingdom of heaven against men; for ye go not in, nor suffer those who are entering to go in." Jesus curses the priest because they shut up (hide or obfuscate the teaching) the kingdom of heaven (which is Jesus' way of saying "bliss"). Let's get one thing straight. When Christ talks about us entering the "Kingdom of Heaven," he is not talking about a place made of clouds and white robes that "good people" go to when they die. He is talking about a state of mind called bliss, which you can enter once you become liberated from the ego.

247

Christ continues, "For they go not (they don't practice enlightenment and the liberation that follows) nor do they suffer those who are entering to go in (nor do they teach the purpose of life to the people who come to them for the teaching)." In Matthew 22:2-4 Jesus again warns people about religion: "The scribes and Pharisees sat down in Moses' seat (as teacher). All therefore, whatever they bid you, do and observe (you followed them blindly) but do not according to their works, for they say and do not (they talk spirituality but don't practice nor embody it). For they bind heavy burdens and grievous to be borne, and lay them on men's shoulders, but will not move them with their finger (they frighten people with damnation bullshit). They love the first place at the feast, first seat in the synagogues, and greeting at the market of Rabbi, Rabbi (they orchestra this bullshit in order to be admired and for their ego's social recognition). Call no one on earth your father (only you can help yourself, only you can decide to grow, to analyze who you are and who you want to become, only through awareness will you discover what binds you. No one can communicate that to you). And whoever shall exalt himself shall be humbled (pride will cause your fall) and he that shall humble himself shall be exalted" (deny your ego and be liberated).

248

As you may recall Christ was killed by the Romans but at the instruction and behest of the Jewish Pharisees and Priest. Don't blame the Jews. It would happen in any religion, and if Christ appeared today, the current churches would reject him as a heretic. Christ would be on the street preaching that you can all become liberated as he has and the church fathers would be saying that is blasphemy and only the son of God can do such wonders and the rest of us are mere humans who need Christ's grace to get to heaven.

Here is a little story that sums up religion for me. A long time ago there was this man who discovered how to make fire. He realized what a benefit it would be to people so he packed his bags and began traveling from village to village, teaching people how to make fire. The people were so grateful because you could imagine the increase in the quality of life to have a warm hut, cooked food, light, etc. It would be a tremendous gift.

One day the man came upon a new village. He walked right up to the center of the market, sat down, and began his ritual of make fire. He set out some straw and began rubbing his sticks together, etc. Well, a crowd gathered round, including the

249

head priest of the village. When the man created fire the crowd jumped back in amazement and let out a huge cheer. They lifted the man on their backs and marched him around the market. After they calmed down he told them he would return to the market each day and teach anyone that wanted to learn how to make fire.

The priests got together that night and they plotted. They said this man is too powerful. The people adore him. He could demand whatever he wants. He is like a god to them. You saw the way they reacted. So the priests set out in darkness, found his campsite, and snuck up and killed the man before he was able to teach anyone the power of fire.

The next day the people gathered in the square to learn to make fire, but the man didn't appear. They set out looking for him and found his dead body. They were enraged. Who would do such a thing? Then a theory started to circulate that maybe it was the priests. The people recalled that the priests didn't seem pleased with him at the market the other day. The priests got wind of this theory and had to act quickly. So they went to the market and announced that a tragic thing happened to the man of fire. All should pay homage. Therefore, once a week we will gather together in the temple and pay homage by going through the motions of making fire like he did. We will make an altar and an effigy to this great man. We shall make a holiday in his honor, and we shall pray to him. And that is exactly what they did for thousands of years...but with no fire.

Our churches, temples, and synagogues have failed us. They preach exaltation but not emulation of the prophets. They instruct us to worship Christ and the other prophets in lieu of entering the path of enlightenment the prophets have laid out before us. Christ informed us in John 14:12: "I say unto you, he who believes in Me, the works that I do, *he will do also; and greater works than these* he will do" (emphasis mine). Most churches preach that Christ is the only son of God and that the rest of us are some kind of lesser creation worthy only of worshiping Christ. Our salvation is not something we are in control of but gifted to us once we believe in Christ and worship him.

This position is not supported anywhere in the Bible. How is it that we can do "greater works" than Christ, if we are lowly un-empowered lesser humans? Christ did not come to inform us he wanted to be worshipped. He came to teach us the path of enlightenment. He did not want churches filled with people mindlessly saying "Lord, Lord," but rather he came to teach us how to make fire, how to become liberated from all sorrow and enter bliss. The church fathers either don't understand the path Jesus taught, or worse, they understand it and don't teach it because they egotistically want us to believe they are the mediators between us and salvation. They lose all their power if you figure out the truth that you can do the works that Christ did and greater works because you too are a "son/daughter of God" and need no one to become enlightened. You only need the will to follow the path that Jesus and the other prophets instruct us to follow: kill the ego and become free.

The only good thing I can say about religion is that it does pacify people's fears. Most people are not emotionally ready for the path of ridding themselves of their ego. Most people do not want to do the work. Very few want to take on the challenge of confronting the ego and the challenge of finding a new source of happiness even if that new source is 100 times better. Like I said earlier, it is so difficult for us to admit when we are wrong, to include the excluded or say that we are sorry.

It is right there in plain English all over the Bible, yet 99% of Christians claim they are not capable of entering bliss because only Christ can perform these miracles. They believe Christ is God, they are lowly sinners, and that they are not capable of becoming liberated but rather it is their job to sit there looking pathetic while Christ does it for them.

How many times does Christ tell us that *we*, not some priest or him, must act in order to "save" ourselves? Almost every sentence of the New Testament starts with "You must" or "Don't..." Who do you think he is talking to? He is laying out a road map for us to see the harmful effects of our ego, a vision of true love, how to avoid the pitfalls of religion, how to grow, etc. Yet the average Christian thinks all Christ ever said was go to church, be a good Christian, and believe in Christ and you will go to Heaven when you die. How the hell did this happen? This is insane. Christ never said any of those things. This is what egos want us to believe and what the priest's ego wants people to believe, but it is the exact opposite of what Christ taught.

This is why I hate religion while at the same time I'm grateful that people have a place to go to placate their fear of death and immobilize them with dogmatic morality in order to keep them from running around the world killing each other out of the fear of the unknown. There is plenty of killing going on in the world under the guise of religion as it is, but at least most religions are teaching people this is bad while you sit in their pews and learn nothing about the prophet's teachings on enlightenment. In my mind this is religion's only redeeming quality. They pacify the fearful and thereby keep them from bugging the shit out of the rest of us.

Psychology, on the other hand, is an essential part of the enlightenment process. The path of overcoming your ego requires the analytical mind of the philosopher to turn inward upon the psychology of self. As the Bible has instructed us, "Man know thyself," and as Father DeMello used to instruct, "turn the light of observation inward." He used to say, "We all love to criticize everyone around us, but only a few of us are capable of putting that type of attention inward upon ourselves. That is the person that is aware. That is the person that deserves admiration."

Remember the psychologist who was called for assistance and upon arrival finds the patient in a pit of human excrement up to his chin? The doctor reaches in to grab the patient's hand to pull him out, and the patient says no, no, no, I don't want you to pull me out. I just want you to show me how to keep it from getting deeper. This is a great illustration of why enlightenment is not the norm. The problem isn't the study of psychology or the philosophical science of observation. The problem, typically, is that people don't want to be healed. We want to make life bearable not fearless. My main criticism of the field of psychology is the fact that, in general, they are not teaching people to question the fundamental problem of the ego. I believe modern psychology is attempting to assist people with refining the destructive parts of their ego so to replace them with more affective egotistical traits. They are not addressing the problem of living life through an ego but are of the position that the ego you are using is poorly structured for the happiness you are seeking. They may say "let me help you create a more affective ego for the job at hand."

I don't think this is all bad. In order to create a more affective ego you must first become aware of what parts of your ego are causing the problem. This is the practice of self-awareness required if you ever hope to become enlightened. The only problem is that they don't know that you must take the next step and question the effect of not having an ego at all. In general, the field of psychology is unaware that you can observe the ego from the vantage point of a being outside of the ego. They are of the school of refining a dysfunctional tool where enlightenment is about discarding the dysfunctional tool for no tools at all.

Enlightenment requires a willingness to observe and a desire to see one's faults. All of us have the option to grow through pleasure or pain. The odd thing is that most people choose pain. We don't question how to improve our relationship, job, being a parent etc. until there is a problem. People don't naturally wake up and practice self-reflection. We don't want to do the work of analyzing our life, applying what we see and making improvements. It's all "too much work."

You know what is a lot of work? Not working on improving ourselves and thereby being in a relationship where our spouse grows tired of our selfishness, loses respect for us due to our laziness, and feels alone due to our detachment. Waiting until they are so unhappy that they become angry at us and then for us to do the least amount possible to get them to stop nagging us. That is a lot of work. This is how the average person lives his or her life. This is how life remains stressful and unfulfilling. I know people in relationships who argue all the time and then, like clockwork, every three months they have a big blow up. Minor adjustments are made to make the relationship tolerable, old habits, which were temporarily hidden, reveal themselves again, and then they have another blow out. This goes on for years.

Wouldn't it be easier to spend a little effort to change? We have the choice to grow through pleasure or pain. Oddly enough, most people choose pain. Typically, we do not confront, challenge, or adjust our present way of life until enough problems arise that require change. As mentioned earlier the old philosophy of "If it ain't broke, don't fix it" and "let sleeping dogs lie" and "don't rock the boat" are the cause of a lot of life's misery.

We have all witnessed this mentality in those who stay in a relationship with someone they no longer love or remain in the job that bores the hell out of us. Typically, these people stay in that relationship until they or their spouse either has an affair or falls in love with someone else, or they stay at that job until they are either on the verge of getting fired or so miserable they are calling the Peace Corps again. Not only is this philosophy the cause of much of our unhappiness in these specific issues, but likewise it is also entirely responsible for the well-known phenomenon called a mid-life crisis.

The problem is that we are not proactive about our happiness. Therefore, we wait until we are unhappy before we start searching for the life that will make us happy. We have all been that person or have dated a person we knew would not attempt to grow until confronted regarding the current state of unhappiness. This is the "growth by pain" consciousness. We glide through life until the negative repercussions of our past acts make our present life so unhappy that we must search for a better way. The epitome of this consciousness is the alcoholic who will not stop drinking until they "hit rock-bottom." The milder example is the person just mentioned who will not work on their relationship until their spouse yells at them. This is growing through prodding or the cracking whip of unhappiness.

The alternative to this consciousness is the proactive person who grows via observation and example. These people consciously observe their actions and the negative repercussions of their actions and thereby make adjustment to their life in order to stay ahead of the unhappiness caused by the build-up of negative repercussions from their destructive acts. These people grow through the knowledge and desire to remain happy and non-offensive to themselves and their loved ones.

Initially it appears that the problem is laziness, but it is a combination of laziness and ignorance. This is another classic example of how ignorant we are about how to find happiness. I call this the why-are-you-always-nagging-me syndrome. Picture your typical guy who just came in from mowing the lawn on a Sunday afternoon. He stops by the frig and grabs a cold beer and makes a beeline for the lazy-boy recliner. He clicks on the tube and begins to flip through the channels. Just then his wife/girlfriend/significant other comes home from running some errands. She quietly walks by and makes her way up to her bedroom. They haven't been getting along that well lately.

At that point our hero does not turn off the T.V. in quiet reflection to figure out what needs to be done to improve his relationship. Instead he is thrilled she didn't stop and initiate one of those "why are you such a jerk conversations." At this moment he is in the depths of his ignorance regarding how to find happiness.

His near-sightedness has blinded him from the knowledge he needs for lasting happiness. Because he is only interested in considering his present comfort and not his lasting happiness, he refuses to see the future repercussions of his present actions. At that moment, there on the lazy-boy, he actually believes he would be happier sipping his beer and flipping through the channels than going up to his spouse's room and inquiring how they can improve their relationship. This is ignorance.

This relationship will have brief moments of happiness inspired by strongly resisted spurts of growth. These rare moments of growth have only been endured through near relationship-ending unhappiness instead of conscious attentive learning and inspired life adjustments.

His ignorance is in his belief that, "If I sit here and watch T.V., I will have the pleasure of being presently entertained. If I turn off the T.V., seek out my spouse and initiate a conversation along the lines of 'honey, I feel like we're complacent, and I want to know what you think we could do to improve our relationship' then I will be imposing mental and emotional labor upon myself. This, he reflects, would be work. Work is not fun. Watching T.V. is fun. So the answer to what will make him happy is to watch T.V. WRONG!

Eventually, because the troubles in the relationship have not been addressed, they remain indifferent towards each other, uninspired, and their sex life dwindles. Eventually the shit hits the fan, someone has an affair, or they are forced to make temporary changes to improve their relationship right before it fails. This is growth through pain and unhappiness.

If we only had vision. That should be the Mantra for humanity. If we only had the vision to see far enough into the future to envision the future consequences of our present way at addressing life we would do better. If we did, we would confront the issues in our life (unresolved relationship issues, failing career

261

choices etc.) which are not fully satisfying our needs in that area. I'm not saying every lazy person would suddenly jump off the couch and finally arrange to meet the long-promised marriage counselor, but I do believe they would more consciously observe and address the issues in their life prior to life becoming nearly unbearable.

We can grow two ways: through the pursuit of happiness or through the escape of unhappiness. You can only stay ahead of your unhappiness if you consciously analyze how your present acts may have negative future ramifications. This can only be accomplished by farsighted vision. This vision requires thinking and contemplating.

You can only image the positive repercussions of this proactive approach to life. In the relationship example alone the amount of happiness added to their lives is astronomical. The mere fact of being in a relationship with someone who cares enough to try as opposed to the typical sloth on the couch would be a dream to most people.

This, "thoughtful life" is essential to become enlightened. This is a process whereby people build a "mature" ego before they attempt to chop it down. What I mean is, we should have a certain amount of psychological stability before we can enter the path of enlightenment. We should conquer a certain degree of fear, obtain a certain degree of self-confidence and personal satisfaction, etc. As candidates for the rigors of the spiritual path I see people who are not overly cocky nor extremely wedded to their ego. They do not possess extreme fears and thereby are not searching desperately for relief. The candidate already realizes the ego isn't the answer to everything. They have already taken steps to refine their relationship to it. They are capable of apologizing, empathizing, are curious, have shunned superstitions, and, lastly, want more purpose. Typically, these people are relatively happy, stable, inquisitive but smart enough not to engage in conversation with idiots because, as they say, don't argue with an idiot as they will only drag you down to their level and beat you with experience.

There are many levelheaded and intelligent people ready to enter the path of enlightenment, but, until now, they have had no pillow on which to lay their heads. There are no institutions that can guide the emotionally mature toward the next step toward enlightenment. Well, this is the place for them. The path of enlightenment does not require membership, an institution, a building, dogmatic rules nor lifelong external instruction. Let life become your teacher. Once you realize the goal is to rid yourself of the ego, you need nothing but the ability to pay attention, the willingness to admit its flaws, and the desire to push away the destructive behaviors right in front of you. That's it.

Two side notes: People have stumbled upon enlightenment out of complete depression or loss of self-identity, but it is a dangerous path that typically leads to psychosis or suicide. I prefer a thoughtful, analytical exploration of happiness instead. On this path not only is the destination a beautiful place, but you can enjoy the journey.

Also, regarding prayer and meditation. Yes, they definitely help. They will help you focus, remind you to take some time to reflect, and they will teach you some emotional discipline, etc. All of these things are helpful in building the muscle of constant observation, which is required to see all of the ego's tricks. Are they necessary? Probably not. But they sure do help. The best prayer is the one that makes the most sense to you. So shop around, try some from various religions. I hope I don't need to mention that God doesn't give a shit which religion you use nor if you use them at all. That would be pretty "egotistical" of him.

Also, remember that religion is a boat and life is the river. It doesn't matter what kind of boat you use. It can be a yacht or a raft. Who gives a crap? As long as it gets you across the river of life to the other shore of enlightenment, it was the right boat. When you get there you abandon the boat anyway. It was just a vehicle. I love the expression that your religion is the ass you ride to the fest. Once you get there you disembark and leave it on the curb. You don't ride the ass into the house for dinner. Non-attachment. Liberation. The enlightened focus on liberation. The non-enlightened compare methods.

We're All Going to Heaven

A priest walked into a pub, indignant to find so many of his parishioners there. He rounded them up and shepherded them into the church. Then he solemnly said, "All those who want to go to heaven, step over here to the left."

Everyone stepped over except one man, who stubbornly stood his ground. The priest looked at him fiercely and said, "Don't you want to go to heaven?"

"No," said the man.

"Do you mean to stand there and tell me you don't want to go to heaven when you die?"

"Of course I want to go to heaven when I die. I thought you were going now!"

Teachings of Father Anthony DeMello

CHAPTER TWENTY-ONE

Azure and I found a one-bedroom apartment in Marina Del Rey. We didn't have much money, so we both started looking for work right away. It was August 2001, and the economy was okay but not great for job searching. I wasn't sure what I would do but wasn't too worried. I applied for an in-house counsel position at a few places because you can do that without being licensed in the state, but no one felt my six months' experience at some cult in Montana was the background they were looking for. Imagine that. I also applied for some paralegal positions but was told I was over qualified, and they were afraid I wouldn't stick around. Azure got a job at a Cuban restaurant by the beach. Everyone assumed she was an aspiring actress because she was way too pretty to not be an actress in L.A.

September 11, 2001 came and went with all its tragedy. After the country woke up from its nightmare I realized I was not going to find a legal job for a while so I better go do something. I was writing most days, but that wasn't paying the bills, so I went back to what I knew I could do. I got a job driving a cab. This was no easy feat. I had been in L.A. for about a month. L.A. is a really complicated city to learn in a couple of days. Passengers were a little startled when they got an English-speaking cab driver and then again by the fact that I didn't know how to get "downtown."

Soon I learned that Hollywood was my favorite place to drive. It was always busy, and if you got a ride to the airport, it was $35 bucks, and on occasion you would get some kids from the 'burbs who had their car towed and needed an $80 ride back to mom and dad's. Those were the rare "normal" rides. Most of my rides were a mixture of locals going to bars, restaurants, and clubs, but the other half of the rides were for prostitutes, drug dealers, pimps, or guys looking for prostitutes and drug dealers. Remember earlier how I commented on the egos in Chicago, the big city, and how it was easier to learn from because they were so bold? Well, being around prostitutes, pimps, and drug dealers is also easy to learn from. It is very easy to be repelled by tragedy. Good grief, those people were living in a scary world. Let me tell you about a couple of my most memorable rides. I once picked up a prostitute who asked me to drive her a block and a half because she was wearing four-inch heels and could barely walk in them. She was a young, attractive Asian-American. I drove her the block and a half, stopped on the corner and told her it would be $4.25. She casually responded by saying, "Hey buddy, I just got on the street and don't have any cash on me. Can I just blow ya for it?"

To which I respond, "Oh, no thanks. It's okay; I got this ride."

To which she said, "Hey, thanks a lot," in a tone as if I really was being generous.

Another time I got a call in the middle of the afternoon for a pick up at a nice house in Santa Monica. When I pulled up two very pretty, very busty, and very under-dressed women jumped in my cab. They were wearing matching, completely see-through nighties with nothing on underneath except for a thong. After they gave me an address I started to drive. Then curiosity got the best of me and I asked them, "I'm sorry to ask, but why are you two naked?"

269

One of them responded, "We're actresses and we just got off the set," and the other said, "We're not actresses; we're porn stars," and they both giggled.

Another evening I picked up this pimp right on Hollywood Boulevard who looked as if he just walked off the set of a '70s movie as a pimp. I swear to God he was wearing a purple velvet hat with a feather, huge lapels, a bright yellow shirt, and white leather shoes. At first I thought it was a joke. He had a bottle of whiskey in a paper bag and ordered me to drive slowly down Hollywood Boulevard at 2 a.m. and stop at every street corner that one of "his girls" were working so he could "talk" to them. The conversation pretty much went like this:

Pimp: "Hey, Bambi, if you don't have my fucking money by 4 a.m., I'm gonna come back here and kick your fucking ass."

To which she would reply something to the effect of, "Fuck you, Tyrone," or "Go fuck yourself, Tyrone," or "Eat this, Tyrone" (accompanied by the appropriate body grab). All involved seemed to be so used to this banter that I assumed it was a nightly ritual. Tyrone did not tip.

My favorite transvestite was this 6'5" guy who made little effort to look like a woman. I would pick him up at least a couple times a month along Hollywood Boulevard. His hair was always a mess, he sometimes had a dark five o'clock shadow, he wore high heels and a dress, but made no other effort to look like a woman. I think his name was Stanley, and when he sat in the back of my cab he talked like your normal Joe. All the other transvestites go to great lengths to act and appear to be a woman. Not Stanley. It was too much of a bother. We would talk sports, and he would throw me five bucks and say, "Have a good night," and walk up to his apartment as awkward as a 6'5" dude in heels should.

I don't mean to make light of the lives of these people. I am mentioning it because they shocked me. I drove people high on meth making no sense at all. I had a passenger ask me to help him pick out a pretty prostitute because he had bad eyesight (we had to interview five different prostitutes through the window of the cab until he found one that was actually a woman. He was picky.).

By day I was trying to write a book on spirituality and by night I was a chauffeur in hell. It was a very, very strange year but incredibly enlightening. I was amazed how complexly dark some people can become. You hear about horrible people on the news doing unspeakable things, but to be alone in a car with them at 2 a.m. and to feel their presence is really creepy and telling. You can feel their hell. Some of these people were tragically lost in a myriad of psychological problems, while others were completely overtaken by very "dark," complex, and extremely self-engrossed personalities.

While I would sit in the car with them and they would talk to me, I would hold the vision of Buddha in my mind and try to get to that timeless place of bliss with pure "evil" sitting right next to me and trying to carry on a conversation with me. *"Yea, though I walk through the valley of the shadow of death, I will fear no evil: for thou art with me; thy rod and thy staff they comfort me"* (Psalm 23:4). Sometimes I was able to do it. Most times it would take all my might to just not feel creepy for the rest of the night. There are some scary people on this planet.

But this highlights my main theme throughout this book, the reason I have woven my life's story into this book. I realized, through these events, that in order to reach enlightenment, the understanding that your ego is the problem, you need to find a great church with the best teacher. That "great church" is the world right where you are, and the "teacher" is life, the exact life you are living. The path to enlightenment is all around us and primarily inside of us. If we are willing to observe the hardship, which is borne out of our current way of living, in ourselves and others, we will understand the problem. Once we realize that the ego's attachments, manipulations, selfishness, and fears are the cause of our unhappiness we will begin the process of casting it out.

The problems of living with an ego are obvious in our actions and the actions of others. Now that you know what to look for, all you have to do is pay attention. Life and all its tragedy will prove the prophets were right. The problem is that we are living through an innately selfish state of mind, the ego.

One bit of caution: don't observe others to find fault in them. We should observe them to find fault in the ego in general and always be cognizant that we are no better than they are. We all suffer the same ailment...the ego. Until we are free from our ego we have no business giving advice to others on how to fix their life. It is the ego that compares itself on a scale of superiority. Our only job is to "fix" ourselves, and thereby we will be doing everything in our power to better the world. As Buddha stated, "Greater in battle than the man who would conquer a thousand-thousand men, is he who would conquer just one—himself (Dhammapada Verse 103).

Isn't this a relief? We aren't here to save the world. The world is perfect in all its dysfunction. The dysfunction is the teacher that will lead us all to enlightenment. Our only job is to find enlightenment, and we have done our part. God has set the laws in motion and placed everyone perfectly in the place they need to confront their dysfunction. She has also given us the perfect tool to escape any calamity: no attachment. We all have the power to stop suffering at any moment we choose, and we have the ability to become enlightened when we so decide.

As Christ said in Matthew 7:3, "Judge not lest thee be judged. Hypocrite, first cast out the beam out of thine eye before and then thou wilt see clearly to cast out the mote out of thy brother's eye." Here Christ pretty much says, "Who the hell do you think you are, judging others while you hold on to the same unhealthy condition." While we allow the ego to control our thoughts we are all just experiencing different levels of selfishness. None of us are any better than the next. Your job it to liberate yourself. Once you are liberated you may give advice to others. Otherwise you will only try to mold them into the person that satisfies your own needs. Your ego doesn't tell people what they need; it is only capable of telling them what it wants from them.

The irony is that once a person becomes liberated, they realize there is very little they can say or do to help anyone. We each must grow sick of the effects of our ego before we will rid ourselves of it. We can't communicate that disdain. It must be realized. Hence the quote, "He who says does not know, and he who knows does not say." The teacher can only point the student back to self-observation. The answer to our suffering is there. It is apparent in every statement that the ego influences and every reaction from the world that filters back through the ego. No one can tell you the affect your ego is having on you. Your ego will not allow that information to get through its interference. Only you can see that from inside. Only you can come to that realization. Your ego would never let someone else convince you of its bad influence. It has too tight of control over your ears, your eyes, and your thoughts.

It's Me Not You

To a disciple who was forever complaining about others the Master said, "If it is peace you want, seek to change yourself, not other people. It is easier to protect your feet with slippers than to carpet the whole of the earth.

Unknown Author

CHAPTER TWENTY-TWO

Love, what is it and why are so few people truly experiencing it? Christ explains it perfectly. In Luke 10:33 Christ states, "love is like a lamp" and in Matthew 5:15 Christ states, "Neither do people light a lamp and put it under a bowl. Instead they put it on its stand, and it gives light to everyone in the house." What he is saying is that true love radiates out in every direction to all in the world. The liberated radiate love without questioning or demanding from those who receive it. Love is not selective. In Matthew 5:43-48 Christ states, "You heard love thy neighbor and hate thy enemy but I say love your enemies for He (God) causes the sun to rise on the evil and the good and sends rain on the just and the unjust. Be ye therefore perfect as your father in heaven is perfect." He tells us to let our love be perfect, which means to be wholly without judgment and without conditions.

Love as we experience it via the ego is everything but non-judgmental and unqualified. The ego defines love as that strong emotion it experiences when it meets someone who it strongly believes can fulfill its selfish needs. This is obviously the opposite of what Christ was talking about. The ego cannot love. It can only barter and trade. It is saying, "I will give you what you need as long as you give me what I need." It is offering a business relationship.

Love, as Christ informs us, radiates out in every direction not because you are currently giving me something but because love simply radiates. Love is already whole. It doesn't need anything in return. You can tell if your "love" is a business transaction because it is qualified. Can it be turned off? Will it end if the person it is directed at ceases giving you something? their love, their affection, their attention, your comfort?

Did you ever meet someone who was so in love with another person that they married them and then when the marriage ended, they hated them? "Of course," you may say. "We all have." It is actually so common we find it normal. This is so messed up. I'm sorry, but how did we get here? How is it not so obvious that this isn't love but rather barter and trading my needs for your needs? Let's call it what it really is: I'm missing something in my life and so are you, so if you will fulfill my needs, I'll hang around. In return I'll fulfill your needs, but as soon as you stop fulfilling my needs, I'm out of here.

Let's be completely honest about how selfish this endeavor is. There is nothing selfless, unconditional, nor perfect about it. This is not love at all. It is perfect in its predictable selfishness. Anyone who is surprised when that "loved one" turns on them the moment they are not getting their selfish needs met is an idiot. I'm sorry, but the only "love" in this world of egos is for sale or trade. The ego doesn't give anything away without payment.

As Christ warns us in Luke 6:32, "For if ye love those who love you, what thanks have ye? For even the sinners love those who love them. And if ye do good to those who do good to you, what thanks have ye? For even the sinners do the same. And if ye lend to those of whom ye hope to receive, what thanks have ye?"

I love the parable that love is like the shade tree. It gives shade to the good and bad all the same. Even the man that comes along with an ax to cut it down. The tree shades this man while he chops it down, and after he cuts it to the ground the tree leaves a fresh scent on the ax. Beautiful. This love is perfect. Unqualified. Given without a need or demand for anything in return. Like the candle in the room, it just radiates out in all directions to everyone in the room without judgment and without a demand for payment.

The ego is incapable of this perfect, non-qualified expression. The ego only knows its own needs. When we let the ego run our life and control our thoughts, we are only capable of barter and trade but not love. The best we could possibly experience is the strong emotion of really, really wanting someone because if I could have them in my life I could have the companionship that I need and am currently missing in my life.

This isn't love. This is an attempt to fulfill a selfish desire. The only reason why the person falls for it is because their ego sees us as the one who can fulfill their void. When this happens the fireworks of the perfect business deal goes off. We are in love with the acquisition of an item that will fulfill a lot of my presumed emptiness. Then it gets worse. Then the game of controlling this source of happiness can begin. I have an idea: let's create an institution called "marriage" so that leaving me will be more difficult and my happiness more secure because it cannot flee on a whim. In addition, I can always withhold what my loved one wants in order to reel them back in when they seem to be taking back too much control over my happiness or their life. I can always use physical pleasure as a way to entice them by giving them what they want in order "to reward the dog" and withhold my affection if I think I need to punish them for not giving me what I want. Wow, this "love thing" is tricky, but once I get to know them I will figure out a way to manipulate them into giving me what I want without even thinking about it. And, of course, if they stop giving me what I want, I'll call them a bitch, call the cops on them, get a restraining order, use the kids against them, empty their bank account, and never talk to them again...because I love them.

Hopefully, I have made my indelicate point that the typical person does not experience love. It is a quest to fulfill *our* needs. Real love has no need. It simply radiates out in every direction without a demand, request, or judgment of any type. It simply is...love.

What is love?

Take a look at a rose. Is it possible for the rose to say, "I shall offer my fragrance to good people and withhold it from bad people?" Or can you imagine a lamp that withholds its rays from a wicked person who seeks to walk in its light? It could only do that by ceasing to be a lamp. And observe how helplessly and indiscriminately a tree gives its shade to everyone, good and bad, young and old, high and low; to animals and humans and every living creature – even to one who seeks to cut it down. So this is the first quality of love; its indiscriminate character. This is why we are exhorted to be like God, "who makes his sun shine on good and bad alike and makes his rain fall on saints and sinners alike; so you must be all goodness as your heavenly Father is all goodness." Contemplate in astonishment the sheer goodness of the rose, the lamp, and the tree, for there you have an image of what love is all about.

Teachings of Father Anthony DeMello

CHAPTER TWENTY-THREE

In the spring of 2002, Azure and I traveled to Montana to visit family for a few days, and I asked her to marry me. To my great delight she graciously accepted. Still to this day she is the kindest, prettiest, happiest person I have ever met.

After being held at knife point once and after getting in a fight with a drunk firefighter who was a passenger in my cab, I thought no matter how much I was enjoying driving a cab and the *great pay*, I was done with this tragic freak show. I decided it was time to use my degree, so I started an on-line real estate closing company out of my apartment in L.A.

Within a couple of months I realized the company could grow and that I would need employees. Azure and I had our wedding planned in the spring in Montana. We decided to move back to Bozeman because we knew having kids would come soon, and there are few better places to raise a kid. We could be around our families again, and it was a great place to find employees due to it being the home to Montana State University. Within a year and a half I had forty-five employees and was making a very good living. Over the next couple of years, we built a house and had two beautiful children, Aiden and Ellyce.

Since the amazing experience of falling into timelessness in Denver, I have wrestled with holding that vision and mentality with varying degrees of success through rigorous theological debate, falling madly in love, driving "Ms. Devil" in Hollywood, through starting a challenging new business which exploded with growth, through my first experience with wealth, and, lastly, while raising kids. I really feel God is preparing me to be able to discuss this crap with almost anyone.

In 2013, I sold the closing company along with the sales and marketing company and retired in order to share my thoughts on enlightenment. I started and failed at a half dozen other companies. I own a pub in Bozeman, MT and have since started two new internet companies with some friends. All along this journey my spiritual path never left my mind. It is not an either/or proposition. You don't turn on spirituality. You don't become religious on Sunday. I started and ran businesses while watching my ego attempt to grow, act, engage, and thereby reveal itself. I came to realize that life is our church. There is no better place to become spiritual than every moment of life. There is no appropriate time to shut down your analysis of the effects of your ego. I don't care if you are in a church or at a cocktail party; observe, question, and analyze why you are doing what you are doing, see the unhappiness that occurs due to your and other's reliance on the ego. Never allow the ego to convince you there is a time for observation and a time to stop observing. Every waking moment is an opportunity to grow.

Life and spirituality are the same thing. Don't have two worlds. Don't have the "now I'll think of spiritual things" world and the "now I can't think about how to improve myself because I'm in my work mode" world. You are not too busy to grow. You are never too busy to analyze your ego. You don't have to go anywhere to be spiritual. There is nothing more spiritual than what you are doing right now. Living life is the most spiritual endeavor available. Talking to a stranger, going to school, getting a job, falling in love, making love, having children, casual socializing are all incredibly spiritual activities. Each one can teach us so much more than reading the bible about who we are, what are our attachments, our fears, insecurities, regrets, desires, and all the other aspects that make up the destructive ego squeezing us like a python every moment of our life.

We must lose our shame and our fear and find the courage to be crude-fully honest with ourselves. We will see that our ego is the problem and that life without it leads to fearless, unbridled bliss.

Impermanence

*A traveler visited the famous rabbi. He was astonished to see
that the rabbi's home was only a simple room filled with books.
The only furniture was a table and a bench.
"Rabbi, where is your furniture?" asked the tourist.
"Where is yours?" replied Hafez.
"Mine? But I'm only a visitor here."
"So am I," said the rabbi.*

Unknown Author

CHAPTER TWENTY-FOUR

You may recall that earlier in this book, I spoke of two powerful spiritual experiences that propelled me forward in my understanding of the ego's effect on my life. These experiences helped me understand how my addiction to my ego blocked my ability to find happiness by keeping me in constant fear. The first experience was in 1989 when I was camping in the mountains of Montana and I had a vision of a house that turned out to be a representation of me. In that house, I found two beings living in the basement. One was an abused child and the other an abusive beast. Both were me. The child turned out to be my soul or true self and the beast my ego. The two lived as one mind with competing goals and hence my conflict. From this experience, I got a glimpse of the enormity of my ego, its influence over my every thought and a very graphic depiction of the pain it was causing me.

Then in the summer of 2000 while driving through Wyoming on my way back to Colorado I had a vision while recalling my behavior at a picnic the day before in Bozeman, Montana. I observed my ego's selfishness with such clarity that it sickened me and I was torn free from it for several days due to my repulsion. I fell into a timeless and fearless state due to the distance I felt from the ego and its attachments and desires. Over the next few years I slowly fell back into a life where my ego felt free to reintegrate itself with my thoughts, but each time these monumental experiences occurred the attachments were lessened and the ego's flaws more apparent. For me, it has been a slow methodical process of acting, observing and learning. Keeping a constant eye on the ego's impact on my decisions, the outcomes due to that effect and to my life overall. As I stated earlier, I used to notice the negative effects years later, then months later, then weeks later then days later and then moments later and sometimes in real time. This is the path toward liberation. Enlightenment is the knowledge that I am the cause of my own unhappiness and liberation is ridding myself of that cause.

I just had my third, and most important, spiritual experience to date. Today is January 12, 2017 and I'm reflecting over my internal debates that have commenced daily over the past 14 months. I have lived in a raging battle with my ego over its fear. Most of the time, which is hard to admit, I bathed in its fear as if we were one. Many times, I stepped out of the bath by arguing that it is its fear and not mine but in hindsight I was so hooked on the fear that I never left the bathroom, so to speak. It had tremendous negative effects on my psychology for the past 14 months. I finally stepped out of the proverbial bathroom and back to a beautiful day of fresh air for the first time in a long time and it may be the most liberating thing I've been able to accomplish along my path.

In order to explain how this event occurred, it requires some facts and some important background information. I mentioned earlier that in 2013 I sold my closing and marketing companies but I did not disclose the amount. Well, that has now become relevant. I sold them for approximately $18,000,000. Remember, just 12 years earlier I was driving a cab in Los Angeles and had $40,000 in credit card debt and $140,000 in student loan debt. Upon the sale of my companies my life changed quite a bit financially and what I couldn't admit to myself was the fact that so did my reliance on the life it created. Not only did my financial position grow exponentially but so did my attachment to the life I created with that income; my ego's pride for its "success," for the attention and admiration that came from others, its pride from its perceived reliance of my loved ones upon the security and comforts they've grown accustomed. You have heard the biblical quote "It's easier for a camel to crawl through the eye of a needle than for a rich man to enter the kingdom of heaven. Matthew 19:24. There is some scholarly dispute regarding what Christ meant by "the eye of a needle" but less controversy regarding his warning to the rich man.

Wealth is the greatest toy the ego could possibly acquire. With wealth, we can buy things which bring us comfort, survival, pleasure. We can buy admiration, fame, "friends." How many rich people do you think harbor some fear of losing their wealth? My guess, all of them. Well, I was clearly one of them. I constantly lied to myself and would say "money added pleasure but was not the source of my happiness." I would proudly point to the fact that I lived most of my life poor and therefore could do it again with ease. I did not want to admit that I had grown attached to my wealth. I am also afraid that I would not have been able to admit that unless a serious and credible threat came along to take it all away. The threat did come, it was real and the result was amazingly liberating and the reason why it happened was equally amazing.

Remember when I stated that most people worship the devil and not God. I believe this to my core. I had been worshiping the devil regarding my finances. I wanted so badly for the status quo to remain, even at the expense of growth and liberation. That is the devil's offer. Worship me and I won't rock the boat. I'll show you how to avoid turmoil in exchange for complacency. God, on the other hand, doesn't give a crap about your comfort. God wants only your liberation. God is not afraid of tough love. God realizes that our propensity is to buy into the fear and to hang onto what we have. To turn a blind eye to our faults and opportunities to grow. In these events God shakes us and when that happens it is up to us to turn it into either a powerful spiritual experience or our worst nightmare.

For the last fourteen months, I labeled the experience, that I am about to share with you, as my worst nightmare. I now realize it has been a gift of God's intervention to wake me up from the trance my ego had me under due to its fear and my attachments.

As I mentioned, back in 2002, I started a real estate closing company. In 2006, I started a non-profit which provided property owners an avenue in which to donate their ownership to charity. It seemed like the perfect fit. I found thousands of people who had an asset they no longer used and now they had a great way to put that asset to great use. From 2006-2013 I raised over $4,000,000 for charity. Who could possibly have a problem with this? Who could get mad at the genius who found a way to turn these unwanted lemons into lemonade for great charities like the American Cancer Society, Feed the Children, Alzheimer's Association, etc.? You guessed it, the Internal Revenue Service. They didn't like the tax write off the donors were taking for donating their property to charity.

So, in 2012 they decided to come after me and the charity. After exchanging over three million documents and spending hundreds of thousands of dollars on legal fees the IRS determined that the charity paid too much money to my for-profit companies for the support services they provided to the charity. The crazy part of this is that they never found any proof that the charity was over-charged for the services provided. After several years of investigation, they never bothered to call competitors to find out what they would have charged the charity for the same services or they did and they didn't like what they found so they never published those findings. I did this survey for the IRS and it confirmed that my company undercharged the charity approximately 50% for the services provided. I shared it with the IRS but it had no effect. I don't think they cared about being right. They wanted to limited tax write-offs. So, the charity was ordered to shut down in December 2014. But the IRS wasn't satisfied with just that. In November 2015, the IRS asked the Department of Justice to sue me in order to get an injunction against me. An injunction is an action whereby you ask a court to prevent someone from doing something. Although they already shut down the charity they wanted to prevent me from doing this in the future. After spending another $150,000 on attorney fees trying to convince the DOJ that this lawsuit was completely unnecessary I agreed to their injunction because it was simply a waste of money to fight for the right to do something I haven't done in over four years and had no plans on doing again.

After settling with the DOJ the IRS decided to sue me for $8,500,000. You may think, "Well you sold your company for $18,000,000 you can afford it." Well, not necessarily. First, the buyers are paying me off over ten years, so I haven't seen most of that money yet. Secondly, the money I have been paid I had to give 46.5% of it to the IRS already in income taxes. If I can't pay it they said they will take everything, my house, my possessions, all my savings and all my income for the next 10 years.

I truly feel that the IRS either knows that they are wrong legally or they simply don't care. They seem to feel that the ends justify the means and if they can use their unlimited resources to shut down, even a legal, avenue to tax breaks, then they were justified. They don't care about the human carnage along the way. When you sit before these attorneys they seem to enjoy inflicting the destruction.

So, I am living on the edge of financial ruin. Which ironically is the greatest thing that God ever did to me. This brings up several amazing theological phenomena. I believe that God stands back and observes us moving toward liberation until we get stuck. I was stuck. I became so blinded by my attachment to my wealth that God realized that I wouldn't see it unless he gave me a push. His messenger just happened to be the IRS. Like I said earlier, God doesn't give a damn about your comfort. God cares only about your growth toward liberation. If the devil had his way, the IRS would have never come along to rock my world and scare the shit out of me. That was God's doing. The Devil would have found me a great investment to further purchase my devotion to the school of financial bliss and all its lovely attachments and underlying fears.

The lawsuit, and who is right (me) and who is wrong (IRS) for that matter, is not the important issue. The important issue is the devastating effect of attachment and the debilitating effect of fear. As Buddha taught us, when you are attached you are suffering. You are addicted to that thing. You believe you can't be happy without it. You fear losing it. The best experience that you can achieve is a sense of pleasure from having that thing layered with the fear of losing it. That is as far as attachment can bring you. That is why Buddha said, and I'll summarize, all the world is suffering due to desire. We are all attached to the things we enjoy and believe we need and therefore we are all suffering because with attachment naturally comes the fear of loss. Therefore, all the world is suffering from the fear of loss.

I lived in constant fear these last 14 months. If the DOJ and the IRS weren't on my door step here to take it all away I never would have admitted it. I would have gone ahead with my life walking around preaching non-attachment unwilling to admit my attachment. A week ago, I got so sick of being afraid that I "spit it out". That is how it felt. Like that time in the woods when

I saw how ugly my ego was and the time in the car in Wyoming when I became so sick of my ego's actions. Once again, it took becoming so sick of experiencing the fear that I found the impetus to step away.

After meditating on it I looked up to God and said "you're right. Take it. Take it all. Take everything that I'm attached to." You know what? I already lost it anyway. Remember once you are attached you killed it. You have a layer of pleasure on top of a cake of fear. You must give up the attachment now to start to live again and to be free and to live in peace and get back on the road to liberation. I now awake every day and beg God to take away whatever it is that I'm attached to…even life itself. I imagine getting the legal judgment for far more than I could afford and it used to cause a panic within me and now I laugh. I imagine being told I only have a month to live. I imagine becoming maimed. The loss of my beautiful wife and amazing kids. I constantly run through all the things that used to scare the shit out of me and I honestly view my reaction. I used to run from the thought and now I hear the ego cry out and I feel the liberating distance caused by the realization that it's the ego's fear and not mine. I no longer want to live in fear. Bring it on. Seriously, bring it on. Free me from myself. From my stupidity. From my attachments so I can start to enjoy every moment. Turn this life of fear into a blissful life of fearlessness and joy. That is my prayer. God test me every day. Take away my attachments. I'll dance this dance with you and I thank you for the liberation it brings me and the pain and death it brings to my ego and ignorant attachments.

This brings up the terrifying question; Do bad things happen or is "bad" a label we put on an event when it challenges our attachments? If you are planning a picnic and it rains and you are disappointed, it is because you wanted to have a picnic. It isn't the rain that is bad. Rain doesn't' cause disappointment. The farmer nearby may love the rain and would have been disappointed if it didn't rain. Therefore, the act is not bad but it's our tightly held expectations that cause us to label the event as bad. Let us take the extreme situation and see if my theory holds up. Being unjustly sued by the IRS with little power to prevent them from taking everything you own would seem universally bad. But it isn't. It is simply an act. It is my attachment that causes me to label it good or bad. For fourteen months, I labeled it bad and it negatively affected every moment of my life both while I was awake and asleep. I could not escape it. I lived in constant fear. That fear taught me the most valuable lesson.

Events are just events. They don't cause fear nor unhappiness. Our attachment causes the harm. Non-attachment results in liberation. Regardless of the event. Someday we will all get the news of our death (if sudden we might find out after the fact). Either way, we will be confronted with the loss of all that we hold dear. All our attachments will be challenged. All that we wish to possess will be taken away. This is the gift of life. This is the way God set up existence in order to wake us up to the stupidity of our attachments. Life is transient. Let it all go now so you can enjoy life while you have it. If you hold on you will never truly enjoy any of it. Your joy is capped at some pleasure layered on top of fear of loss. That is the best that the ego and its attachments has to offer. Do not spend the rest of your precious life in fear. Embrace non-attachment. Become fearless and all the wonder and beauty of life instantly becomes yours.

Is that so?

A beautiful girl in the village was pregnant. Her angry parents demanded to know who was the father. At first resistant to confess, the anxious and embarrassed girl finally pointed to Hakuin, the Zen master whom everyone previously revered for living such a pure life. When the outraged parents confronted Hakuin with their daughter's accusation, he simply replied "Is that so?"

When the child was born, the parents brought it to the Hakuin, who now was viewed as a pariah by the whole village. They demanded that he take care of the child since it was his responsibility. "Is that so?" Hakuin said calmly as he accepted the child.

For many months he took very good care of the child until the daughter could no longer withstand the lie she had told. She confessed that the real father was a young man in the village whom she had tried to protect. The parents immediately went to Hakuin to see if he would return the baby.

With profuse apologies they explained what had happened. "Is that so?" Hakuin said as he handed them the child.

Unknown Author

CHAPTER TWENTY-FIVE

The meaning of life is to become enlightened and to use that knowledge to gain complete liberation. Remember, that to be "enlightened" means to understand our manufactured id (ego) and its attachments are the cause of all our suffering. I don't just mean read about it. I mean meditate upon it to the point that you KNOW it. You have witnessed it. You understand your ego is the devil blocking you from true happiness and infinite wisdom. You understand that you and it are so intertwined that your thoughts, while reading this line right now, are primarily being interpreted by your ego and that your ego will most likely tell you what you are going to do with this information.

The enlightened assume they are not in control and that the ego is trying to block their spiritual path, hijack it, and redirect their attention toward some useless mindset (religious fanaticism, intellectual pride, etc.) in order to save itself. You must want to see it. You must want to get over your addiction to it.

Always remember the liberated feeling you got when you thought about never giving a damn about being accepted by anyone again. If you felt the elation, the liberation, then you have the ability to see the harm your ego is doing to your life at this very moment.

Remember, the best tool to help you see your ego on a daily basis is to *constantly* say, "Why did I decide to upset myself just then?" If you can say this every time you become upset, then you will continue to drive that wedge deeper between you and your ego. It forces you to question the ego's effect on your life. It forces you to view the ego from outside of it as opposed to viewing life with the ego's mind. You must constantly turn the floodlight upon the insanity of the ego's control and childish ambitions. This practice will give you a new non-ego-based person to observe it and life from. It will empower this new person every time you observe and reject the ego's reaction.

Christ, Buddha, Lao Tzu, and all the other saints and prophets came into the world in order to wake us up to our true divine, fearless, blissful potential. There is a powerful story that describes this awakening: There once was a lion that was separated from his pack shortly after birth. He wandered off and mixed in with a heard of sheep. He ended up growing up with the sheep. He ran with the sheep, grazed with the sheep, and lived amongst them all his life.

One day while he was out in the field grazing with the other sheep a lion leapt out of the jungle and gave chase to the herd. He was about to pounce on one of the sheep when he saw this lion running from him in fear with all the other sheep. The lion from the jungle gave chase and soon captured this cowardly lion and said to him, "What the hell are you doing running around with these sheep."

The lion replied, "Please don't kill me, Mister Lion. I'm just a harmless sheep."

The jungle lion was confused, so he said, "Come with me." He took the frightened young lion into the jungle to a pond, and he said, "Look into the pond and tell me what you see in your reflection."

The young lion peered into the pond and was amazed at what he saw. All his life he believed that he was a powerless, fragile sheep. But in his reflection he saw a mighty, powerful lion.

After staring at his reflection for a couple of minutes the young lion stepped back, lifted his head, and gave out a mighty roar.

This is what Christ and the other prophets came to do, to wake us from our illusion of mortality, weakness, and powerlessness. As we tell the alcoholic that their first step is to admit they have a problem, in spirituality, our first step is to realize we have unlimited potential. We must realize there is no difference between us and Christ, Buddha, Lao Tzu, and all the saints and prophets throughout time. Believe in your potential to live life with NO fear, with NO attachments, and with true love that flows out of you in every direction like a mighty river with no need to receive anything back because we are already complete.

God, whatever it is, wants one thing from us...our liberation. You have heard of the amazingly spiritual visions I have had along my trek. Those were not reserved to me. They are waiting and available to anyone who is willing to make the effort. God, through his messengers (Buddha, Christ, Krishna, Father DeMello, etc. etc. etc.) is nearby. These beings have entered my life on numerous occasions and have given me the tools to make the next step. They want so badly to assist us, but nobody can make you want to wake up to the truth. Only you can. Nobody can make you enlightened. Christ can reappear and before the priest, ministers, and preachers killed him again he could scream from every church and synagogue, but that still won't make anyone enlightened. Only we can do that. We must want it. We must find the desire to get out of the bad marriage with our ego. Our ego is a childish, self-centered maniac that has hijacked our mind, our life, and our happiness. What are you going to do about it? It is time to wake up and become enlightened.

I'm going to retell the story about the wandering mendicant and the precious stone. At some point, if we are to succeed, we must embody the bravery and the wisdom of the villager. Here it is.

There lived a poor man in a village in India. He lived in constant anxiety due to his poverty and wished so badly to be wealthier. He was convinced that if he just had more money, almost all his troubles would be gone. One day he was walking to town, and he saw a traveling mendicant, which, in India, is a homeless, wandering sage or enlightened man. This traveler was sitting under a tree, enjoying a bit of relief on a hot sunny day.

While passing the mendicant he noticed him holding a large shiny stone. He was curious, so he walked closer, and to his shock it was the largest diamond he had ever seen. It may even have been the largest diamond ever discovered. It was most likely priceless.

He walked right up to the man and stood there staring at it in awe. The mendicant looked up and saw the man's expression and asked him if he wanted it. The man replied, "REALLY? You would give it to me? It may be worth a million upon millions of rupees.

The mendicant casually responded, "Sure, no problem, take it. I found it in a cave that I slept in last night. It's all yours."

The man was so elated he grabbed the stone and ran home with it. He sat in his little hut and planned on how to sell it, and he thought of all the things he would do with his new-found wealth. After many hours of planning he began to think about how it was that the mendicant was able to give away the stone, all its wealth, and all the things it could buy. He went to sleep with that thought, and in the morning he packed up the stone and headed out. He went back to the place where the mendicant spent the night, walked up to him, and said, "If I give you back this stone will you teach me the fearlessness which enabled you to give it away so freely?"

The meaning of life is to become enlightened to the fact that all unhappiness comes from our association with our ego and belief in its attachments. We must realize that life without the ego is a timeless, fearless, blissful existence. Once we are enlightened we will naturally desire the ego's destruction, which will result in our liberation. Enjoy your journey.